# Experiments in Renewal

Edited by ANTHONY J. WESSON

with *A Theological Critique*

by DAVID E. JENKINS

London EPWORTH PRESS

1971.

Enquiries should be addressed to:
The Distributors, The Methodist Book Room,
2 Chester House, Pages Lane, London N10 1PZ


Made and printed in Great Britain by
The Garden City Press Limited
Letchworth Hertfordshire SG6 1JS

*To all who seek*
*the Renewal of the Church*

# Acknowledgements

THE AUTHOR and publishers are grateful for permission to quote from the following:

*Letters and Papers from Prison*, Dietrich Bonhoeffer, SCM Press Ltd, 3rd revised edn. (1967); *Sociological Year Book of Religion in Britain No. 3*, ed. David Martin and Michael Hill, SCM Press Ltd (1970); *Studies in Church History, Vol. III*, ed. G. J. Cuming, Cambridge University Press; *The Evolution of a Community*, Peter Willmott, Routledge and Kegan Paul Ltd; *Homes for Today and Tomorrow*, Her Majesty's Stationery Office; *New Society*, New Science Publications; *Value Systems and Social Process*, Sir Geoffrey Vickers, ABP International, Tavistock Publications Ltd.

# Contents

# *Preface*

THIS BOOK had its origin in a suggestion made by Harry O. Morton at 'The Renewing Church' conference held at St. Peter's College, Saltley, Birmingham, in 1968. The aim in publishing the book was to bring together descriptions of experiments proceeding in the churches in Britain today. No attempt has been made to cater for only one brand of churchmanship, denominational allegiance, or theological conviction. Contributions were invited through advertisements in the leading religious newspapers, and by invitations sent out to people known to the British Council of Churches to be engaged in experimental ministries.

Some of those invited to contribute declined for various reasons. For some the experiments were not at the stage when publicity would have been helpful, for others it was not possible to reduce the material available to the size required by the limitations of the book.

This does not pretend to be a description of all the renewal experiments going on in Britain today. It simply represents work proceeding from a variety of viewpoints. I hope that it will stimulate more experimentation, and much more discussion.

I would like to express my appreciation to Canon David Jenkins for agreeing to read the manuscripts and contributing a theological critique. His action in doing this represents for me a parable of what theology is—reflection on action in the light of one's convictions regarding God's revelation in Jesus Christ.

If this book contributes but little towards the longed for renewal of the Church, then the labour will have been worthwhile.

*Rochdale, 1969*                    ANTHONY J. WESSON

# Introduction

THIS COLLECTION of papers describing various renewal experiments indicates that there is still a large amount of vitality in the Church. Clearly, in some areas, the reports of the Church's death are exaggerated. It is hoped that in those areas where there is much more substance to such reports this book will be read, pondered and acted upon. There is a sense, of course, in which the future of the Church depends upon God's will, but that fact can only be accepted as a word of comfort when everything possible has been done to make the existing institution a fitter instrument for God's purposes.

One aspect, at least, of the process of secularization which has relevance for the Church at the moment is the changed attitude towards history and the future it has brought about. Secular man no longer thinks of history as a prearranged plan of events unfolding before his life and revealing his place in the total picture of human existence. Rather is the emphasis upon man's responsibility for creating the future. This I believe is the essential meaning of man's maturity, and, further, it is a dangerous though precious gift given to man by God. In terms of Church renewal it carries with it the call to face the living issues of the day, and in the light of the truth given to us by God, to take those decisions necessary for creating the new Church of the future. No emphasis on the work of the Holy Spirit, however right and crucial it might be, must be allowed to sidetrack the Church from facing the relevant issues and making urgent decisions. To refuse to live in the world God has created by retreating to the womb of religion is nothing short of unbelief.

There is no reason why the Church should lose her nerve. The fact that this has happened is an indication of the theological unpreparedness of her members. The simple fact is that many people in the Church do not have the requisite resources to make sense of the contemporary world. Consequently the impact of contemporary life is received as a threat rather than as an opportunity. The religious area of life provides for many people the one last bastion of unchanging security in a rapidly changing world. No wonder then that Church people react with uncharacteristic vehemence when fundamental changes are proposed in the life of the Church. But to preserve security in this way is to preserve the security of a corpse. The people of Israel, in the midst of their harrowing experience of the wilderness, asked for a sign from God. They received the manna which fed them, and which was a sign that God would never desert them. The one condition attached to the gift was that they should only gather enough for the day. Owing to their lack of trust in God they tried to garner enough for the future. They tried to preserve that which God said would be given fresh every day. The result, in the vivid words of the Authorized Version, was that 'it bred worms and stank' (Exodus 16:20). The same theme finds expression in the New Testament concept of discipleship, where to find one's life one must first lose it in carrying the cross (Matt. 16:24f.). That is the lesson that the Church, as well as her individual members, must learn afresh in our day. Without constant renewal, and the gathering fresh every day, Christian experience and institutions breed worms and stink.

I find it rather disturbing that Christians should so easily be pushed off their balance by the contemporary world. Clearly the work of contemporary theologians, which represents a massive and impressive attempt to respond to the challenge of the secular world, has not permeated the greater part of the Church's life. Indeed, the claim, that the biblical faith in the living God of history is one of the major factors producing this contemporary world, is now well established. If then God is so involved in the life of this new world why should Christians tremble with such fear? We need to take fresh courage! We can stand with Bonhoeffer and claim that '... the world's coming of age ... is now really better understood than it understands itself ... on the basis of the Gospel and in the light of Christ' (*Letters and Papers from Prison*. Letter dated, 8.6.44). It was that conviction, and the knowledge that it could be justified which gave to him the courage to withstand the degrading horror of fascism, and to die a matryr's death convinced that death was for him not the end, but 'the beginning of life'. It is only such conviction, and the knowledge that it is not an empty claim, which will enable the Church to find the necessary liberty to enable renewal experiments to proceed. The only security for the Christian is in Jesus Christ—not, most certainly, in relative, historically conditioned Church structures and organization.

There are some Christians who would be impatient at the time and energy spent on Church renewal. They would have us believe that their energy is better directed to the concerns of the world, and that the Church must limp along as best she can. This, I believe, to be profoundly mistaken. If one believes that the Church has a message to proclaim to man, as well as a service to perform for him, then the renewal of the Church must be taken with utter seriousness. It is a fallacy to assume that the majority of people will be able to see Christ and respond in discipleship without dealing with the dimming, distorting, even destroying lens of the Church. One of the most serious obstacles to the proclamation of Christ and the development of a community arising from that proclamation, is the image of the Church which many carry. Attempts must be made to change that image if the word of Christ is to have free run among the mass of people. This book gives some indication of how that problem is being tackled.

Throughout these descriptions certain themes recur. It is worthwhile summarizing them here.

First, there is the constant emphasis that mission involves service to the community. It is impossible to think of the Church in the world without seeing it as a serving presence. Other bodies may serve mankind, and in so doing may be indistinguishable from the Church. That, however, in no way detracts from the fact that the Church *must* exist as a serving presence, since the fundamental reason for her existence is the claim that the love revealed in Jesus Christ is basic to human life. Love is that reality which must be demonstrated primarily in action; love that is talked about without being lived is an empty emotion. Furthermore, the love seen in Jesus Christ is that which extends to man irrespective of man's response. In spite of all their protestations of loyalty, the disciples fled from Jesus at those critical moments of his life. His love for them did not cease. It is against this background that the pressure in the Church to justify the spending of time and energy and money by showing an increase in numbers supporting the Church, a pressure which is clearly present in the situations described here, must be seen as a faithless response. The simple fact is that in most parts of the country the Church has to win the right to be heard, and that is going to be a costly business. At all costs the temptation to run to a religious hideaway must be resisted. There are secular men, who would think of themselves as unbelievers, who nonetheless face the naked reality of life without retreating; dare the people of God do less?

Second, there emerges the clear call for the establishment of ecumenical churches. Yet, at the same time, the difficulty in creating such structures cannot be evaded. Not only is it becoming increasingly clear that parish and circuit boundaries are irrelevant to mission in an urban society, since many significant aspects of life are lived outside the residential base, but, in addition, the differences of theological principle and ecclesiastical organization cherished by the denominations are inapplicable to the changed conditions of the twentieth century. Those people who seek to further the cause of their own denomination must face the question, 'Do you really expect modern secular man to come to Methodist, Anglican, Roman, Congregational or any other denominational church?' If the answer is 'yes', then this marks that person out as someone who has not yet begun to appreciate the significance of secularization. The fact is that, in the secular century, the denominational differences are not matters of absolute truth, but expressions of relative historical perspective.

To be seriously concerned about the renewal of the Church today is to be committed to the creation of ecumenical structures. What is urgently required is a 'bridging operation' at the grass roots level of the churches' life to enable the move from the present denominational churches into the ecumenical church to be made as speedily as possible.

Closely allied to this is the third theme, that of stewardship. This, however, must not only be interpreted as a call to the individual members of the Church to live by the principle of stewardship, but much more a challenge to the denominational hierarchies. Personal observation would lead me to conclude that the most faithful members of the Church are giving as much as they can in the face of mounting economic pressures. There are fewer really wealthy people prepared to give the amounts that have been given in the past. Acceptance of a proper sense of stewardship by the denominations would involve them in at least two decisions. In the first place, it would mean deciding that money must be directed into men rather than buildings. Some buildings are clearly necessary, but in terms of mission today properly trained and equipped men are far more important. In the second place, it would involve the decision to trim the hierarchies and organizational levels of the Churches' life to the barest minimum, so that the maximum number of men are released to operate at the grass roots level. The tragedy is that the trend appears to be in the opposite direction.

The fourth theme raised by these papers is the crucial role of the laity in the Church. This has been a theological commonplace for at least two generations in all the denominations. Here we see that theological insight more than justified by the practical experience of mission. The key to the future of the Church lies clearly in the development of lay initiative. This is obvious as the Church moves more and more into community service. It will also be evident if the Church takes seriously her calling to be the revolutionary people of God, aligning herself on the side of the poor, under-privileged, and the political prisoner. The encouragement of such lay initiative raises the critical issue of the development of a proper partnership between minister and layman. Such will only be pos-sible when the minister recognizes the expertise of his lay people, and through work-parties and the like, provides the structures whereby it can find expression. Another facet of this issue is that of the place of the charismatic individual. In today's society with its increasing emphasis on specialization, such individuals tend to be an embarrassment and destructive of genuine team work. Un-happily too many of our churches are structured round charismatic leaders. The problem for the future is to build structures primarily for teams, but which are flexible enough to allow the charismatic individual to emerge, and which mitigate the worst effects of such individualism. Clearly this is going to involve a revolution in ministerial training, amongst other things.

There are three elements that I would like to have seen much more in evidence than they are, in the papers contained here.

Whilst there is involvement in local political and community affairs there seems to be a lack of awareness of the global dimen-sion of contemporary life. Modern man lives in a global village, though the consciousness of the majority is largely limited to their own locality. The Church, in her official thinking on mission, is very much aware of this fact. The traditional division between over-seas and home missions, though it may be perpetuated for organiza-tional reasons, is irrelevant. The mission of the Church is now world-wide. It is as pressing in Western, secularized cultures, as in Asian, African, and Latin American cultures, which are only just feeling the impact of this process. The Church has a crucial role to play in keeping this global dimension constantly before the local community. Its relevance to the problems of race and world poverty is obvious.

The descriptions here raise the issue of how seriously the denom-inations are committed to mission. Supposedly the Church exists for mission as a fire exists by burning. Yet many of the experiments are struggling through lack of adequate financial resources. Is it not time for the denominations to take their commitment to mission much more seriously? To do this, however, would involve transferring resources now used to bolster up failing causes into experimental situations. If this is to happen then work ought to be concentrated into the main conurbations where people live, so that there can be an adequate base from which to work. It would also involve taking seriously the results of the experiment and building upon them. No scientist would conduct an expensive experiment then ignore the results simply because they did not coincide with his preconceived notions. Yet this state of affairs is not unknown in the Church.

Finally, most of the experiments here recorded operate from a denominational base and seek to bring people into that fellowship or community. Clearly such a tactic is going to have a limited appeal in the future. There exists a sizeable number of people who, having withdrawn from the present institution, nonetheless retain a living and profound interest in the Christian faith. What I would like to see is the development of work amongst people such as these as complementary to the efforts to renew the present institution. My own experiments through action groups indicate that people are prepared to respond to the call to meaningful action— as long as this does not mean spending time and money in propping up church towers and maintaining redundant buildings! Such groups would be doubly worth-while if they could be convinced that they have a mission to the present institutional churches, not for what they are, but for what they can become.

It is the conviction that the Church can change and become a more adequate expression of the Gospel than she now is, that enables many people, lay and clerical, to remain in her ranks. I hope that this book will give such people fresh courage and hope.

# 1. Change, Experiment and Unrest in Moss Side

MOSS SIDE is an inner-suburban area of Manchester, two miles SSW of the city centre, and covering about one square mile. It was built 120 years ago to provide good housing for the upper-working, and lower-middle, classes of the time. In contrast to the very superior areas of Whalley Range and Victoria Park with their large houses standing in spacious grounds, Moss Side was built in rectangular patterns, with two- or three-floored, terraced houses predominating. Until the Second World War the area retained its character very largely, but since the war it has become more and more dilapidated, until now it is a slum. The growth of the large council estates of Fallowfield and Wythenshawe, providing more modern accommodation for rent, together with the increasing repair-costs of older Moss Side housing meant that the sort of people who had hitherto found Moss Side an attractive place to live in no longer did so.

Since the war there have been successive waves of people entering Moss Side, attracted by the comparatively low prices of the houses, and by the less restrictive rules applying to rented accommodation. The first of these groups were the Irish, who had to find new areas to live as the even older property in Hulme and Ardwick became sites for inner-city demolition and local authority redevelopment. During the war a considerable number of mid-European refugees came to this country, and many of them, principally Polish people, settled in Moss Side. The third influx was of coloured immigrants from the Caribbean and Asia. But had not a single coloured person come to Moss Side, the problems presented by the age of the housing, and the need for low-rent and low-price accommodation would have been experienced. The pattern in Manchester has followed the pattern in most other cities: that decay travels from the centre of a city outwards, followed by renewal of demolished areas.

Within this general framework, a more detailed picture can be seen. The social composition of Moss Side is interesting and important. The first group are those who regard themselves as 'Old Moss Siders'. They are indeed, many of them, old in years. In their younger life they struggled and sacrificed in order to be able to buy their houses, and they were rightly proud of them. Many of the old people in the area inherited the houses they live in from their parents. Their memories have tended to become overlaid with nostalgia about the past. They remember Moss Side as they thought it once was; and they resent the changes that they are being subjected to. They tend to focus their discontent on any new group of people who come to live near them. The Polish and Irish are remembered with greater kindness now that coloured people are providing the latest focal point of their resentment. Unlike younger people, who can aspire to leave, even if yet they do not do so, the older residents know they have no hope of leaving for more attractive areas of the city. They can hope for a flat in a new housing area, but to move to a council flat is even more disturbing than the changes they already feel themselves subjected to. They tend therefore to ask merely to be left alone, and are fearful that they may not be able to cope with the uncertainty that the future holds for them.

The second group are those, generally working class people, who have been trapped in the area by the rapid change which has come over it in the last twenty years, and who are unable to move out because of the restrictive prices or restricted availability of other housing; or whose businesses, mainly small shops, demand their presence.

The third group are the immigrant people, mainly coloured, who have moved into the area in the last fifteen years. According to a recent social survey[1] about 35 per cent of the population of Moss Side are coloured. Of these, by far the greatest proportion are from the various Caribbean islands. They tend to live near to people from their own islands, and attend churches according to their national origins. Thus the Jamaicans support the Moss Side Baptist Church and the Leeward Islanders Great Western Street Methodist Church. This pattern is now beginning to break down, as some of them, by saving or other enterprise, are able to buy or rent better

[1] Robin Ward on the religious attitudes of coloured people in Moss Side (Manchester University Department of Sociology, 1968), cf. *Sociological Year Book of Religion in Britain No. 3*, ed. by David Martin and Michael Hill, SCM (1970), p. 12ff.

accommodation in areas adjoining Moss Side, such as Chorlton, Whalley Range and Victoria Park. The Asians, mainly Pakistanis and Indians, are not very numerous in Moss Side. A much greater proportion of them live in adjoining areas. But there is a Sikh community, who seem to prefer to move into the area, or remain in it, because their temple, in Monton Street, is the centre of their cultural, as well as their religious, life.

Of all the immigrant groups, the West Indians are not only the most numerous, but also the most restless. They are in the unfortunate position of having had the greatest common cultural heritage with the English, but at the same time feeling themselves rejected by those who, they had been taught, had a special relationship with them. Being Christian, they expected a welcome. Having a common language, they expected no difficulties of communication. Having a similar educational system, they expected their academic and trade qualifications to enable them to be at an advantage over other racial groups. It would be hard to exaggerate the feeling of hurt and disappointment many of them feel, and there are increasing signs that they have given up the idea of integration, desiring instead to stay as close together as reasonably possible, and ensure their cultural and social comfort and safety by being part of a recognizable community. There is considerable—and growing—resistance among the coloured community to the local authority plans for the demolition of much of Moss Side (Ward's survey shows that it is as high as 83 per cent). The following is a quotation from a letter received in March 1969, from a lady who lives in Wythenshawe, and is used, with her permission, to illustrate the feelings of helplessness and isolation which many of these people have.

I and my family as West Indians well all six of my children are natives of this country.... We have moved to this part of Manchester just over a year and six months now and I am telling you the honest truth it is a very nice place to live, but the people who lives around make me think I am not wanted for you can't talk to them no more than twice if you gets the chance to do; they are not as sociable as my own people, they stick to each other so I stands out when they do talk to me ... they always seems to pick on my children ... [other parents] never come to me and make a complaint they call in the Police for such simple matters as if the child is a criminal. I say when I was living in Moss Side I never had in the Police untill I came up hear....

She then goes on to mention the difficulties she is finding with her six children in a small flat, and the complicated processes which she has to undergo in order to change to a larger one. She continues:

> the council don't want to much coulerd folks to live near each other which I think is not a very nice thing to do because just sticking one in hear and there it makes them feel cut off and lost.... The things I have met with up hear in just a year and a half I never met with in seven and a half years in Moss Side. God Bless that place no matter what other people call it, it comes to me like home now. When I go down to do my shopping and visit my friends I feel so much better. I really feel happy, but when I have to come home it is a different spirit with-in me, but I am afraid we have to live with it or go back to our place of abode when we can. It is only since I came to this country I notice their is two different colours of people in the world ... and [it] make me feel useless and unwanted. Even the Church is not so friendly. Black people is even now growing into the same habit [as] all those who use to attend Church. ... Well Rev. Jackson we all have to pray to God more often and ask him to remove these hatred between nations haven't we?

But an increasing number of West Indians are refusing to turn to prayer as any sort of realistic answer to their problems. They openly accuse the Churches of being fatally compromised with the majority white opinion of England. A number of organizations have grown up in Moss Side which originally were designed as social meetings of people of common home back-ground. More and more these organizations are turning from liberal to radical aims. There is little real danger of breakdown with the normal English institutions at the moment, but the signs are not encouraging. If too many of the tolerant and liberally-inclined are driven to despair of the normal processes of democratic pressure and protest, then there are in existence embryonic, but real, radical groups which they could easily join, and for whom 'direct action' is a political creed.

The fourth category of people in Moss Side are composed of the really depressed social groups. Among them are the inadequate—either individuals or family groups—who seem unable to cope with the ordinary strains and complexities of modern life; those who have responsibilities which they, not unnaturally, find very difficult to meet: single women with children, deserted wives, husbands and young people, men and women with poor incomes and a large number of children; those who are constantly on the move from one city to another, transients with 'no fixed abode', often men, and more rarely women, with criminal records; and the criminally inclined, or those who live on the criminal fringe. It is easy to romanticize this fourth group. They are the ones who give Moss Side its popular reputation among the residents of other and more respectable parts of Manchester. Even to categorize them as a separate group is wrong. They may be members of all the other groups as well. But it is the inadequate, the morally delinquent, the socially repressed, who make the name Moss Side not just a description of a geographical part of a major city, but an emotive term in itself.

## The Churches

The churches in Moss Side present a number of problems: their number, their age, their positioning, their denominational differences and their differing theological and social emphases. John Kent[1] has given a typically caustic review of them:

In a typical area of a northern industrial town, for example, there are between forty and fifty thousand inhabitants. As one moves from north to south through a densely built-up area, with two main shopping streets, scores of sidestreet corner shops, and patches of almost shopless housing-estates, one sees quite a number of churches. Six of these are Methodist, with a paper membership of about seven hundred and fifty, and actual attendance of not more than six hundred. These six Methodist churches are all on one circuit, are grouped in two clusters of three, and one pair is ripe for closure. There are three ministers, only one of whom has a society with more than two hundred members; one other church of the six may be called 'lively'.

The area is contained in six Anglican parishes ... [which] vary from extreme Evangelical to mild High Church. ... There are six Anglican parsons; at least one of the Anglican churches is superfluous by Methodist standards of redundancy. There are also open in the area one more or less derelict Baptist church, two Congregationalist churches, one alive and one dead, and an

[1] John Kent, *The Age of Disunity*, Epworth, 1966, pp. 204f. He does not name Moss Side, but to anyone who has worked in the area the picture is familiar. Kent himself taught at Hartley Victoria College until 1965. He includes in his survey a number of churches which are in Chorlton-cum-Hardy, not Moss Side.

English Presbyterian church whose function is to give religious expression to the residual national feeling of a colony of Scottish exiles.

He goes on to assess the total Protestant population at 3,500; explains that the two Roman Catholic churches in the area perform for Polish, Hungarian and Irish communities the same service as the English Presbyterians; assesses the religious population of the area to be about 10 per cent; and ends his summary by saying: 'I do not think that there exists among either the laity or the ministers any real sense of living as part of a general Christian community.'

When Kent wrote this he was giving, unfortunately, the correct picture of the area and of the churches in it. By 1970 it is unlikely to be correct any more. It is the change which is taking place in those churches, and the reasons for it, which have given rise to this chapter.

There were three problems facing us when we began to think out the role of the local churches some six years ago: what was the future of our Methodist churches in the area? what should be our relationship with other churches in the area? and what should be the relationship of our churches to the community in which we were set? The only practicable answer we could give to the first problem was to sell the present churches and unite the societies in a new suite of buildings on a new site. The answer to the second problem seemed to us to be to attempt to form a new structure whereby other local churches which had hitherto acted entirely apart from each other, or had only expressed a romantic and cosy ecumenism by holding occasional united services, could express a new unity. The answer to the third problem was to see if we could demonstrate the concern of the churches for the whole area by sharing in the support of an essentially secular movement, which came to be called the Moss Side People's Association.

The purely Methodist problems presented by the three Methodist churches in the area need not delay us long; they are entirely familiar. Whalley Range, an ex-Wesleyan church, built in 1869 for the 'carriage trade', or at least aspiring to do so[1], seats 800 and has an adult congregation of thirty-five to forty. It has a lively tradition of good fellowship, mainly among women, and a quite extraordinary record of care for the welfare of the people in the immediate

[1] cf W. R. Ward, 'The Cost of Establishment: Some Reflections on Church Building in Manchester' in *Studies in Church History*, ed. Cuming, III, 277ff.

vicinity of the church, mainly through the parents of the junior church children. It has seen better days, but has overcome its unreal nostalgia for the past and has demonstrated its ability to think in new ways about its worship and mission. Great Western Street, an ex-Primitive Methodist church, built in 1878, is tempted to rest on its great tradition as one of the most important Primitive Methodist churches in Manchester in the past. It served until comparatively recently as the college chapel for Hartley Victoria. Its people are puzzled and worried about the way the area has changed, and have not yet come to terms with its modern role, and tend to be nostalgic for its past glories, and continue to look for that day when a messianic minister will appear to restore its former greatness. Claremont Road, built in 1912 as a daughter church of Great Western Street, and to minister to the Rusholme end of Moss Side was closed and sold to a West Indian Pentecostalist church in 1966; the money from the sale being retained in the circuit for new building in Moss Side. The congregation was transferred either to the nearby Anglican church or to Great Western Street.

In 1966 the Leaders' Meetings of Whalley Range and Great Western Street went away for a study weekend to formulate plans for the future. Their plans were accepted by the churches when they returned, and were that for the future we would need a new centre for the churches' work on a new site as soon as possible; that we should embark on stewardship in an attempt to persuade all those who belonged to our churches of the Christian use of money, time and abilities; and that we should not contemplate building anything until we had consulted any other Christians in the area. Since then the two trusts have been united and regular joint evening services have been held. From a position in which the people were fearful of losing their own places of worship they have changed, and are now impatient with delays in building what they call the 'new church'. Stewardship has been financially successful, but only to a limited degree in other ways. Because of the decision not to build anything without full consultation with other churches, the problems associated with the siting of whatever we build anew have delayed us, and have raised in urgent form the difficulties indicated in John Kent's book. Unwilling to act alone, we have had to await the willingness of surrounding churches, not only to join in our discussions, but to act together with us in a unified ministry to the whole area.

It has been my conviction for some years that before strongly-based new structures in such areas as ours can be formed—as opposed to exciting ephemera—three requirements must be met. Whatever is done must be an agreement between friends, and time and energy must be expended in fostering friendships. The existing structures of church society must be used to the limit before new structures are formed, the old ones having been seen by all in the local churches to be inadequate. (This is confessedly a liberal rather than a radical approach, but holds out more hope of carrying the whole people along as opposed to carrying only a few of them.) And, third, there must be some parity of size, strength and local influence between a group of churches hoping to act together. The triumphalism exhibited by very strong churches over very weak ones in their vicinity can easily be observed in many towns and cities. The temptation of the strong is either to ignore the weak one, or, if it notices the other's presence, to absorb it. The first requirement was met in Moss Side by the growth in friendship of the Methodist minister with one of the local Anglican clergy and the Baptist minister. The second requirement was met by using the local council of churches which these friends resuscitated in 1965. The third requirement was met automatically: none of the local churches was in fact so strong that it could realistically continue for long to ignore the others.

At first we concerned ourselves only with that co-operation which would be possible for our churches without causing too much pain to our people: united Christian Aid work, occasional united services, starting 'Mosscare'—a housing association—and acting in consultation with each other on whatever city and local committees we happened to belong to. Gradually we came to see that if we were not to be trapped in this limited co-operation, we had to move into more adventurous experiment. Our problems were that, although our churches were not far apart in distance—in some cases only hundreds of yards—they were separated by parish boundaries. Although this was not a great difficulty for the Free Churches, the Anglican clergyman could not act freely save in his own parish. The attempt must be made to share our concerns with every church in the area, not with just the few which happened to be congenial to each other. And before we went any further we must invite others to join with us so that, before our ideas became too fixed, they might modify our views as well as allow us to influence them. It was soon obvious that the local Council of Churches would not serve our purpose. It was too coloured by the particular emphases of those ministers and laymen already in it, and the other clergy and laity had rejected invitations to join. Clearly, too, there were many personal as well as theological tensions to be resolved if we were to progress. It was felt that if a new approach were to be made, using official denominational channels, there might be more chance of success.

The Bishop of Manchester agreed to ask his Archdeacon to call into existence a special meeting of all the local Anglican clergy, and to invite to it all the ministers of other denominations. This he did, and the first meeting was held in June, 1968; there were six Anglicans, led by the Rural Dean, two Methodist ministers, one a superintendent, one Methodist deaconess, the Baptist minister and the acting minister of the Church of Christ present. We agreed to a morning meeting every five or six weeks, and resolved to stay together, whatever the theological and personal disagreement we had, for one year.

By December 1968 it was clear that we were making very little progress: too much time had to be spent at each meeting re-capitulating conversations for the benefit of some member who had not been present at a previous meeting, or unresolved discussions had to start all over again. It was resolved that we should attempt to come to some definite conclusions about our real intentions to commit ourselves to each other at a three-day retreat/conference. This was held in February 1969. Our outline agenda was that the first day should be spent in honestly revealing tensions, the second in examining ecumenical experiments in other areas, and the third day spent in trying to formulate outline plans for the future. The Bishop of Manchester agreed to open our conference with devotions, and we asked the Chairman of the Manchester and Stockport Methodist District to conduct our closing act of worship; a difficult task for the latter, as he had no idea until he came whether he would be asked to bless progress or pronounce obsequies.

Much to our surprise we found that our outline agenda was quite wrongly timed. By lunch on the first day it was clear that what we had thought to be serious tensions were not as difficult as we thought. The afternoon of the first day had to be spent in looking at other experiments—but none of them seemed very helpful, as they concerned much smaller or narrower groupings than ours, or were in quite different sociological areas. The second day we spent in vain attempts to work out detailed plans for ourselves, and little was really achieved except that it was evident that there was a real desire to do something in common. On the third day we realized that the most important thing we could do was not so much to arrive at detailed plans as to formulate some document which we could take to our churches and which committed us to each other and to the leading of our people into such measure of fellowship as we had found. The document we eventually produced we called a Covenant. In it we recognized each other's ministries; we determined to act together in the neighbourhood as one; and we recognized that the ministers do not constitute the Church. This last resolution meant that we had, as soon as ever possible, to invite the laity to share with us in such a partnership in ministry that we could indeed become the servants of the Church and the world, and assist both Church and world to maturity in Christ. When we ended the conference none of us was in any doubt that something remarkable had happened to us. Without exception we felt that we had experienced the most significant event of our ministries since ordination.

Looking back now, even only a few months later, one is struck, and slightly embarrassed, by the naivety of what we did. One can only say that at every subsequent meeting, when difficulties and tensions have arisen, that document and the memory of its signing, are what we all turn to as a reminder of our common commitment to each other. Our disagreements now are of a totally different nature than those before. It seems to have provided us with a platform from which to reach out for other good things, and without which little of what we are now achieving could have been attained.

Since the February conference we have concentrated on how to give concrete expression to our unity, and take it out of the realm only of the professional ministry. We arranged to have a staff meeting of the Group each month. Two of us were asked to prepare a reasonably coherent plan so that the church buildings in the area could be made more useful for Group ministry. What we proposed, and what the staff meeting approved was this. That the local council of churches must be kept in existence and strengthened if possible. This would mean that the Group would be able to act in concert together with other Christians who did not feel able to covenant fully with us—chiefly the Roman Catholics and the Pentecostalists. Next, that we ought to review all our property and see how it could best be used for worship and service. The Methodists and the Baptists already had plans for rebuilding. The Baptists had an imminent scheme for building a youth centre, with local authority support. The Methodists were committed to some sort of rebuilding. We suggested therefore that, rather than each church attempting to exercise a full ministry, each church should concentrate on one or two aspects of the work, and hope that fullness of ministry would be achieved through the whole Group. As the Baptist premises were just across the road from St Mary's Anglican Church, and since that area was being replanned by the local authority as a new District Centre, if the Methodists were to build some plant next to St Mary's, then that sub-group could share all its resources for more effective ministry. By building in incompleteness we hoped that denominational barriers would be more easily broken down.

In Moss Side East there are four Anglican parishes, a Methodist church and a Church of Christ. Demolition is not so imminent on that side of the area as in Moss Side West, but it was not too early to begin negotiations with the local authority to arrange for the exchanging of at least three Anglican sites for one new site on which to build a church complex through which to exercise ministry, in partnership with the Church of Christ and the Methodists, all having rights in the use of those buildings. The other churches in the Group are sufficiently far apart to require their continued existence, and to develop special ministries of their own within the Group. If these plans were agreeable to our churches, then this would leave the centre of Moss Side free of churches. But there was felt to be a need for some physical expression of the unity of the whole Group. It was therefore suggested that we build (using Methodist and Anglican compensation moneys) a Pastoral and Administrative Centre. This would be manned by the whole Group, records and office work would be kept there, and it would soon become generally known in the neighbourhood by residents and the authorities that this was the centre, apart from the worship activities, of the ministry of the Group.

There were two other issues of major importance we had to consider. Before we asked our laity to join us in our aims, we must be sure of the measure of support that would be available to us from the authorities of the denominations to which we belonged. We had to impress on them that we were not proposing a new inter-denominational denomination. We asked for a meeting with the heads of each denomination, which they willingly attended. When they heard what we were proposing, and the preliminary financial details were seen to be realistic, the Bishop, the Chairman of the District and the Area Superintendents of the Baptists and the Church of Christ, promised their support, and said that they saw their role as being to support the Group at those secular and ecclesiastical levels at which we had no place, but to which they had free access.

The other crucial issue is that of a constitution. We have been assured on all sides that this is a rock on which many dreams have foundered. Who is to lead such a Group? Is it to be a minister or a layman? What is to be the relationship between the ministerial team and the lay teams? What sanctions can realistically be applied by the Group to individuals and churches that appear to be taking wrong courses? How are we to avoid the dangers of simple federalism? These are very important issues because, if many lay people feel threatened by the possibility of losing 'their' place of worship, ministers tend to react violently against any diminution of their freedom to act as they think fit. No answers have yet been arrived at, but it seems likely from the discussions so far, that if partnership in ministry is to be seen to be a reality in the Group, then the professional ministers will have to be evidently in a serving, rather than in a commanding, position.

The most crucial issue of all up to the present we recognize to be the early and deep involvement of the laity. As soon as the ministers felt that they had a little more than dreams to offer to their people they each asked their Leaders' Meetings, Parochial Church Councils and Deacons' Meetings if they would nominate two or three representatives, who would hear what we had done, and would discuss the tentative plans we had arrived at. This was quickly agreed by all the appropriate church meetings, and three lay/ministerial meetings have been held. New developments are taking place all the time, but at the time of writing there is every reason to believe that the laity are becoming as interested and committed as are the ministers. Indeed there are already signs of impatience with the caution we have shown so far.

It ought to be said that the scheme outlined above is open to many criticisms. Not the least of these is the seeming enthusiasm for buildings as opposed to the provision of a freer ministry through persons. There are probably still far too many centres in the Group for what is, after all, a fairly small geographical area. There is such a wide divergence of theology and polity in the Group that some are afraid that it cannot hold together for long. But what are the alternatives? If we have theological agreement we shall be in danger of only working in very small groups, and remaining permanently out of touch with the seminal thought and the judgements of others. If we proposed too radical a policy over the use of buildings, we should be in danger of losing many of those who may at least through this scheme come to a new view of their part in the total ministry of Christ's Church. What we claim so far is that we have a chance in fellowship to offer to Moss Side such a variety of work and worship as to exclude few, and yet enable ourselves to be more free to move among the whole people of the area and make real F. D. Maurice's claim that Christ died, not for the Church, but for the world.

If we are to provide a church structure which should enable us to serve the world, we have to examine and understand in some detail what this means, both to those who call themselves churchmen, and to those who do not. And learning to do this is a very painful process. It is painful because in order to learn one has to enter into and work with entirely secular structures, and in doing so one is in constant danger of losing the confidence and support of those in the churches who find it difficult to understand what one is engaged in. It is a painful process also because one realizes how protected the ministry is, and how, being in the Church for a number of years makes one form assumptions about the ordinary conduct of secular life which are wildly inaccurate. It is, for instance, very difficult from within the Church to realize with what suspicion, contempt and even bitterness the Church is regarded by many ordinary, decent people; how many offers of help are suspect just because they are offered by someone connected with the Church; with what amusement one's early dabblings in social work are greeted by professional social workers—some of them Christians.

And yet the lesson must be learned, and it is perhaps no bad thing that ministers are being subjected to the pressures which many of the laity have suffered in silence over many years. One wishes that more of the laity had been more vocal, or at least more skilled in teaching the churches what the secular world is all about.

The remainder of this chapter is about how some of us in Moss Side have attempted, and are continuing to attempt, to grapple with this most urgent problem. What is said would not be agreed with by the whole Group of churches in Moss Side, indeed some of the ministers and their churches are opposed to the whole concept of secular involvement. Our hope is that we will teach and check each other as we go along. Principally this side of the work has been attempted by the Methodist, two Anglicans and the Baptist ministers, deaconess and, with some confusion and hesitation, by their churches.

It is necessary to draw a distinction between the work done as individuals for individuals, and work done through involvement with social committees and corporations. The assumption is also made that behind all this work there lies much of the usual work of the churches, principally through fellowship groups, youth work and work among the old and the lonely and the sick. Too much distinction must not be drawn between corporate and individual involvement: the one type of work often informs and helps the other.

Moss Side, as has earlier been shown, is an area which attracts people with all sorts of problems. There are many agencies through which they can seek help, and we have not felt it our proper work to attempt in any way to supplant these agencies, rather have we seen it our business to offer a sort of 'first-aid', to help people to understand their welfare rights, and to join with people in ensuring their civil rights. The longer one remains in a neighbourhood, the more opportunities one seems to have for offering help, always assuming that the help one offers is intelligent, realistic and without religious strings attached. The one great advantage we have, as ministers, is that we are not thought to be part of the official structures; we are not paid by the 'Town Hall', we are not connected with the police and we are not associated with any political party. It is difficult to say how this sort of work with individuals starts to build up. One helps a church member, maybe, and then someone on the fringe of the church, neighbours tell someone you are available to help, and so it builds up. One also fosters any introduction to solicitors, policemen, social and case-workers, doctors, local politicians, voluntary social workers and so on. We also have the advantage that we live nearer to the people than many other workers, and we are available at times when many official offices are closed.

One of the most intractable problems in Moss Side is that of the relations between the law, the police and the coloured people. For some reason an increasing amount of my time has been spent in the last two years in visiting coloured people as soon as possible after their arrest, ensuring that they are treated properly while under arrest, and finding legal help for them when they appear in the courts. It is no business of ours to determine the guilt or innocence of those we see: our work is to ensure that at least they have a respectable and skilled friend who can help them with a service at a time when they feel most frightened and helpless. It is surprising the number of people who have never been in trouble with the police before, and are unlikely ever to be so again, who seem at some point to find themselves under arrest. Above all it is our objective to try to demonstrate the ability of the Church to offer uncompromising and disinterested help. Another great area of need for help in Moss Side is with evicted families; we have, over the last few years built up an ability to offer short term accommodation and introductions to the right agencies for longer term assistance.

The other aspect of secular involvement is corporate. In February 1968 a public meeting was called to consider the setting-up of a social council, which eventually came to be called the Moss Side People's Association. This is not the place to discuss the intricacies of such popular movements: our intention is to show how in Moss Side we have come to see the churches' role in this Association. After a working party, on which two of us were represented, had suggested a simple constitution, a public meeting in June 1968, elected a General Purposes Committee composed of local residents and social workers of various sorts, and two ministers, myself and an Anglican. I was elected chairman, the secretary was the Warden of the Manchester University Settlement, and the treasurer was an extremely left-wing West Indian. The method of working was that the people at the public meetings would express concern over any matter they felt needed examination, and, if the people felt it was warranted, a working party would be set up specifically to deal with that issue, by gathering information, and after discussion with the General Purposes Committee, by finding ways of exerting pressure on the appropriate authorities, meanwhile reporting progress to the public meetings which were held every two months.

As we became more embroiled in the details of investigation of complaints, the gathering of information and learning how and where best to apply private and public pressure, so we were able to report less and less real progress, and what information we were able to give was becoming less interesting to public meetings. The working parties ranged over housing (in which action was stultified by disagreements between the members of that working party), through street-cleaning, library facilities, the provision of nurseries and play-groups, to a social workers co-ordinating committee. Try as we would to keep the public meetings interesting, they were ceasing to attract great numbers. We were ripe for a radical bid for being taken-over. And that is what was tried. Moss Side is not only a place full of problem-groups and problem individuals, it is a melting-pot for many ideologies, mainly of the political left. A group of radical

New Left students, radical trade unionists, together with a sprinkling of West Indians interested in direct action had grown up in the area. They correctly identified housing as the most important as well as the most emotive issue in the area, called a public meeting of local residents, declared a policy of direct participatory democracy, and demanded not only to be allowed to join the People's Association, but to be able to nominate for co-option to the GP Committee a sufficient number of local people from the Direct Action Group on Housing to constitute a majority on that Committee. We called a special public meeting, at which over three hundred people were present, and it was overwhelmingly agreed that housing was indeed what the people wanted to interest themselves in. Since then we have been almost exclusively concerned with this main issue, and the People's Association has effectively changed from being a broad-based body into a narrow, but more militant action group.

What is of interest here to the Church is not to analyse how control of this rather amorphous Association was endangered, but whether the Church, in the person of myself, should ever have allowed itself to be placed in such a position of leadership, or whether it would not have been better to ensure the presence of the Church at every point where discussions about the style of life in Moss Side were taking place. One is grateful for every valuable experience in life. I have had to learn a great deal about the Church and the society in which I am living. There are many lessons staring us in the face today. The disillusion of many coloured people with the ineffectiveness, as they think it, of many councils of community relations; the general cynicism among ordinary people about the normal democratic processes and the integrity of local politics; the manner in which the Archbishop of Canterbury's chairmanship of the recent consultation on racism held at Notting Hill was held to ridicule, should teach us, if we have eyes to see and ears to hear that if we are to be a Church of the people, then we must unlearn much of our triumphalism, we must recognize that Christianity has, as such, no prescriptive right to a place in the sun of popular esteem, and will be judged as one ideology among many, and by its deeds it will be known.

The Church has no *necessary* brief to support any government, or any class, or any sectional interest whatsoever. I now believe, and am trying to put into practice, together with my colleagues, that the Church really must allow the world to write its agenda, and if that agenda at any particular time says 'housing', or 'race', or whatever, then that is where time, energy and prayer must be spent.

Second, I believe that we should ourselves learn, and teach others, especially our laity, to learn that committees (on which we proliferate) have no life and no function of their own which is self-authenticating and self-perpetuating. They must be made to learn to work hard to gather information, analyse facts and opinions, and offer advice which is for the real good of the people they represent. Third, we have come to see that the efficacy of the Church in our generation will lie in its constant care that society is served to the best of our ability, in humility, and warns of the dangers of residing in the claims of sectional interest, and that when everyone else has moved on to new concerns and new foci of interest we will still be there offering alongside every other hope and ideology, the love of Christ.

# 2. The Challenge of a Central Mission

## EXPERIMENT IN GRIMSBY

L O R R I E S travel the country bearing the message 'Grimsby Fish', yet industrially Grimsby is more than the world's largest fishing port. The post-war years have introduced into the area man-made fibres, chemicals and oil refining. In consequence the population has risen rapidly, new people have moved in and the 'natives' have enjoyed a moderate affluence.

The Churches in the same period declined numerically. The Grimsby Methodist Central Hall was no exception. It was founded and opened in 1936, being the amalgamation of three Societies. The original membership was recorded at 350. In 1951 it stood at 327; 1961, 252; and 1963, 205. District Commissions decided to close down and sell up, withdraw from the heart of the port and build elsewhere 'providing a suitable site could be found'. A Connexional Commission discovered that within a matter of ten years the Central Hall area was scheduled to become the largest housing development within the Grimsby Borough. It was decided to stay put. However, the resources available were hardly the best material for new work. The membership had declined over the years and the congregations even more so. The building was in an appalling state. The Hall had been in debt and living on an overdraft for the entire period of its life. A programme in relation to the town was non-existent. The lay people in the main were on the wrong side of sixty and had been exhausted in their attempt to keep the doors open. However, the decision to remain open had been taken and a new minister was appointed. What follows in this report is the description of how the task was tackled, and what we have today in consequence of our efforts.

## Market Research

Our first task was to engage in a careful survey of the area in which we were being asked to work. We needed to know as much as could be gathered about the people who would make up our potential 'clientele'. What were their habits and needs, social and cultural activities? Where did they shop and what kind of wages did they earn? Where did they work and what were their hours of employment?

We discovered:

1. Our people were being rehoused in flats and maisonettes.
2. There were no play areas for the children.
3. Families could be placed mainly in the lower bracket income groups, this necessitating mother having to work to help supplement the finances.
4. Flat tenancies seemed to cut them off from the rest of the town and they had no sense of belonging either to their neighbours in the conventional built houses, or to each other.
5. Shift work affected not only father but mother as well.
6. Social life was thereby affected, and 'family' life almost impossible.
7. In the face of problems there was a reluctance to contact anyone who was 'official'. The war between 'them' and 'us' was a matter of reality for the 'us' group at any rate.
8. Among those who would have sought help there was little knowledge as to who and what was available.

This was the face of our parish. With the facts that this survey had revealed we could at least move into the planning and development stages of our initial work with intelligence and care. It should be added that the assistance of the Local Authority, Welfare Departments and Press was invaluable in collecting and sorting this information.

### The Pew and the Pavement

The principles which were to govern our work had to be clearly established from the outset. These provided a constant subject for education on the part of the church member. It was not that the 'religious' were unwilling to serve others, it was simply that they had been brought up on the staple diet of 'pew fodder', a quick numerical return for effort involved, or give up and conserve what one had. They had not, of course, been taught that such an attitude was certain death! Interminable discussions went on apace with the new work. Always the theme was 'service without strings attached' and this was not an easy fact for the many to accept. To carry the majority it was therefore necessary to begin with them where they were, and not where the leadership wanted them to be. To the established Methodist a rise in congregational numbers is as important, if not more so than the establishment of community work. Therefore, we began both simultaneously. In an attempt simply to move the congregation physically out of their own building they were sent leafleteering. We were aware that this was mere publicity and invitation to services, but at least it was a beginning. The laity, generally much maligned for their inertia, took up the challenge they understood (increase in worship numbers) and followed on to the community service they did not understand with equal fervour and enthusiasm. They responded magnificently to leadership which for them had been a rare commodity. The congregations did increase numerically and have continued to do so throughout the past six years.

**Related Worship**

The 'specials' of any church were first of all used to attract people. However, these were then supplemented in worship that had a local interest: Trafalgar Services, Life Boat Sunday, to mention but two which mean something to a people whose life is spent in a fishing port. Organizations outside the Church were invited to help make these relevant and they responded with genuine interest. Related worship is vital to any local situation. It is ludicrous to hold only a harvest festival in an area where the population have never 'ploughed the fields and scattered the good seed on the land'. It is more to the point to organize for fishermen and a fishing port a 'Harvest of the Sea' or for a totally industrial area an Industrial Festival as well.

Preaching, in a central Mission, is of equal importance. The act of worship given over to dialogue and discussion has its place but preaching in a Central pulpit is certainly not a thing of the past for the man who can deal with it! It is of interest that a group of intelligent teenagers in our local situation have recently made the comment that they prefer a good sermon, providing a man has something to say, can say it in an articulate manner and with enthusiasm and challenge. They did however concede that they were prepared for the sake of others to take part in 'experimental worship'. They knew, however, what they wanted, 'a good sermon followed by discussion and information'. Perhaps it would be as well if we who lead the Church asked what was needful, instead of deciding out of our wisdom what the people must have! However, worship of itself is useless, service must be the natural outcome and we had to teach the church that it was not sufficient to spend the whole of our time with the bread and the wine, but that the towel and the basin must also confront us.

## Pastoral Care

A Sick Visitors Team was established to care for the 'shut ins' belonging to our Church and to no Church. The visits are carried out monthly and reported to a member of Staff who passes on to his colleagues in the Team Ministry relevant information, especially in the case of emergencies. An Action Group to deal with decoration of homes and tidying gardens was put to work. 'Taxis' were made available by private car owners not only to bring the infirm to church if they desired to come (and many of them did) but also to transport the disabled to chiropodists, lawyers, etc. Tape recorded services were taken to those who wanted to hear their own congregation at worship and their own minister preaching. Baby sitting brigades were available for the 'young marrieds' who found it impossible to get out together. The deaconess was housed in the flats on our suggestion and with the co-operation of the Borough Council. On the side of the Local Authority she was classed as a 'key worker', and has carried out an effective ministry among these people with their special needs, but as one of them. All this led to a deeper concern for people and the necessity for pastoral work at a deeper, more personal and protracted level.

## Counselling Centre

The Counselling Centre was opened in the first year of the new programme. Advertisements in the press invited those in any kind of despair to contact the Staff of the Central Hall. They began to come and have continued to do so every day. Our 'clients' are made up of those to be found in any part of the country. Categories are used only for the sake of this report. Matrimonial, hire purchase, financial, alcoholics, methdrinkers, homosexuals, unmarried mothers, adolescents, delinquent parents, suicides, depressives, etc. This side of our work is undertaken by co-operating with Welfare Departments, doctors and voluntary organizations such as the Telephone Samaritans, which we founded at local level, and who are housed on our premises. We are not able to publicize this work and so our people have to trust us for the use of our time knowing that often others have a prior claim on our ministry.

## The Community Centre

Founded in 1963 the Community Centre had very definite aims in view: To provide a meeting place. To offer our premises to those organizations in the community who had no home of their own. To facilitate social needs. To provide the opportunity of caring for people at close quarters. To establish contact with the non-church-goer. To provide a door step to the Church, its life and worship.

Our clubs were established not on the principle of what we thought the people needed, but what they could not do without. The list today speaks for itself: Pre-School Playgroup, Junior Play Hour, Youth, After Eight, Eighteen Plus Clubs for Young People, Men's Association, Women's Club, Senior Citizens, Toddlers, Mothers and Babies, Tufty, Widows Club; all this together with the usual uniformed organizations and specialized organizations, as, for example, a Club for Divorced and Separated people. Affiliated groups include the Tenants Association and Telephone Samaritans. The Centre is staffed by a full-time and qualified Community Centre Officer and ninety-four lay workers. And all this in a church where it was said officially six years ago that there was 'a serious lack of lay leadership'!

The Centre also provides a training ground for local schools who send their Sixth Formers to work in our clubs as part of their civic training. Moreover, the Staff lecture and have contact with the schools on their premises linking our work with theirs in the influencing of young people at school leaving age. Further, Conferences of organizations throughout the County and the Church are held at the Central Hall, so that we might share our insights with others and so that we might learn from them.

## Port Missioner

Loss at sea, the care of bereaved families and aged seafarers must always be the major concern of any local Church in a sea port. The Port Missioner as a member of the Team Ministry carries through this side of the work. This part of the programme was again a matter of co-operation between an outside organization and the Methodist Church. A Port Missioner has worked in

Grimsby for nearly a hundred years but always alone. Today he is part of the Team and shares in the life and work of the Mission as we share in his specialized ministry. His task is to break the news of loss (this occurs frequently, in that the fishing industry has the highest accident rate of any industry in the country). To care for the families after loss. To counsel those families whose father is away for long periods and need help in his absence. To care for fishermen themselves ashore and afloat. He is also associated with an Orphanage for seafarers children and the housing of aged fishermen in the Borough.

## Industrial Chaplaincy

A further extension of the Pastoral work of the Church is the Industrial Chaplaincy. The Chaplain is where men spend the majority of their time at work. Further, his task is to 'uncover truth by conversation, discussion and debate, using his theology as a tool of discovery'. That a Team Ministry such as ours is important to his work is without question. Our Industrial Chaplain believes in being locally based in a local church (if but loosely) and, moreover, based within a Team that is of a community centred type of church rather than of the usual residentially based conventional ministry.

## Christian Community Groups

Education of a continuing kind is essential to our task. Our membership is therefore divided into Christian Community Groups which meet in the homes of our members and are led by trained lay leaders. Biblical, theological and social matters are discussed under the overall leadership of the deaconess. It is through this 'cell' work that new ideas are evolved and new opportunities seen and met.

Lay Commissions have worked over a period of six months examining our work, its strength and weaknesses, and suggesting changes and developments needful to our ministry. In every sense now the Laity are part of the Team.

## The Team Ministry

The Team Ministry has been built up gradually and has been in its present form for the past two years. The basis of its structure has been both the volume of work and the need to have qualified people to undertake the leadership of lay workers. It should be further noted that the Team Ministry has on its membership both ordained and lay workers; we cannot understand a Team Ministry without both.

The Team Ministry became possible because of a definite plan on how to build up the necessary team of workers with the fact of limited finance staring us in the face. The facts are as follows. The Superintendent Minister is financed by the Central Hall. The Deaconess is subsidized by the Home Mission Department on a grant of £400, but reducing at a hundred pounds per annum, therefore, the major part of the appointment is the responsibility of the Central Hall. The Industrial Chaplain is financed in equal parts by the Home Mission Department and a local Society, the second Centre of the Mission. The Community Centre Officer is financed in total by the Local Authority; the Port Missioner equally so by the Sailors' Children's Society.

Without such planning and help no Team Ministry would have been possible and this report could never have been written.

Our plea for extra help and assistance, by way of man power, and financial resources to pay them, has not been met. We understand the difficulties, and in some measure and with impatience accept them. However, the Staff at the present time are working hours and meeting demands that one would not expect many to comply with. The Honorary Secretary of the Mission, for example, is paid a part time wage but works an eight hour day, five days a week.

## Church Structures

Church Structures have had to be adapted to meet the administrative demands of our task. The Mission Committee is that body which combines local and Methodist District Personnel. The Leaders' Meeting is used for the spiritual oversight of the church. Congregational meetings are regularly called for the imparting of information and the opportunity of asking questions. It is not sufficient in our programme simply to consult with the Leaders' Meeting which by its constitution is limited in numbers and personnel. The Community Centre Management Committee has on it representatives of statutory bodies, Church and non-Church organizations. The Community Centre Council is that body of Club leaders who run the Centre from day to day along with the Community Officer.

Of necessity a great number of decisions in our kind of work

need to be taken immediately and without the calling of committees. Therefore, the Team have total authority given to them by
their lay colleagues. This indicates the measure of trust that has
been built up over the past six years.

## Ministerial Training

Knowledge gleaned has not been kept to ourselves, but has been
from the outset shared. The Staff of Richmond Theological College
have worked with us closely from the beginning. They have provided us with man power by way of a Student team and encouraged
the men to enter into a programme of training sessions in order
that their academic work should be related to the practical work of
a local church. Further they have sent men for longer periods of
training so that both sides of this alliance have benefited.

Richmond College apart we have had the privilege of having on
the staff for limited periods visitors from overseas, mostly ministers
who have worked with us to gain insights for their own work in
their own countries. It should not be forgotten either that their
visits have given to us extra help for which we have been more
than grateful.

## Difficulties

The laity in the early days had no clear indication of what we were
about. The truth of the matter was, that not only had they not been
led from the top, they had not been asked either to take responsibility in their own right. Therefore in the beginning a benevolent
dictatorship was essential and accepted. This took courage on the
part of the Staff, in direction and leadership and, moreover, in the
knowledge that what they were doing and asking others to do
might well end in failure at the last. This capability to experiment
to the point of failure is a quality that must be nourished in the
hearts of those who would lead the Church today.

Methodistically speaking it has been difficult to interest others in
our work to the degree of real support. The attitude 'we have our
own place' is tragic but wide spread. Many of our Methodist people
who have our kind of experiment in their District have not realized
that we are not, nor do we wish to be, in competition with other
'ordinary' Methodist churches. Our aim by reason of our building
and staff is to extend the ministry of the Church with a capital C.
Within this view it should be possible to help other Churches and
be helped.

It would be regrettable enough if the views one hears expressed against ones work were confined to the laity, but the Ministry is not without blame. In our experience we have had a great deal of support and encouragement from a few ministers; the majority have been interested, but have not lent support, save to use the Staff for the addressing of meetings and rallies. In the case of a few, whose influence unfortunately outruns their numerical strength, the criticisms have been more in the form of an attack rather than in the spirit of a well wisher! Comments regarding the number of staff as per the number of churches, Connexional grants (the amounts are always exaggerated by the uninformed) the apparent 'freedom' we enjoy outside of normal Church structures, these show a lack of understanding of the nature of the work undertaken and a 'sour grapes' spirit. It would be my hope that the long and traditional battle between 'Churches' and 'Missions' could quickly come to an end so that the real work might go unhindered by obviously dedicated men on both sides.

Financially our position has been intolerable. It will be quickly pointed out that we have received help and this is true. The facts are as follows: The building was in need of total redesigning. Grants were awarded to us by the Rank Trust and the Chapel Department. Funds for this project were also raised by Trusts that had sold up, and from the Ministry of Education and Science. However, this left the local people with something over £2,500 to raise for the capital project. A new manse was purchased for the Superintendent Minister because the former house was totally unsuitable for modern needs and economic management. The debt of £800 between the sale and purchase prices was left for the local congregation to raise on a free interest loan. The overdraft at the outset stood at £2,500. After a struggle while raising money to start the new programme and pay off the overdraft £1,000 was given to us as a gift by a private donor. Nevertheless £1,500 was again the responsibility of the local people. The Central Heating had to be renewed, a burden that could not be foreseen even by professionals at the time of the redesigning of our premises. The cost of this (£1,400) has only been undertaken by a further loan at 5 per cent interest over five years from the Chapel Aid Association.

In total summary out of a budget of £10,000 a year, and including the grants outlined elsewhere in this report, this still leaves the local membership of 220 to raise moneys in the region of £7,000 per annum. Thus funds have of necessity to be raised outside the Mission, because no local group of people can be expected to support alone a programme instigated at the wish, and carried out in the name of wider Methodism. This fact necessitates the Superintendent Minister being involved in a round of fund raising and outside engagements in this country and abroad, wherever fresh but limited sources of cash can be discovered. This in itself weakens the Team for while the Leader is away from home his work has to be covered by others. No criticism is intended, but we have an earnest plea that some plan for realistic subsidies by the Methodist Church might be evolved so that work such as ours might not only be started but continued.

Ecumenically it has not been possible for us (apart from the Industrial work) to link with other denominations in a concentrated work. This has not been for the want of trying on our part. We have initiated discussions in an attempt to share the burdens involved and to extend the work further. However, one of the major denominations could not join with us because of the rigid structures of their own organization; the other would not, because we were not regarded as being high enough up the 'Churchmanship ladder'. This may well lead us to believe that a great deal of education will have to be carried out with the Ministry at grass roots level, before ecumenically based work can be carried out as a norm rather than as an exception.

This account has been only a thumb nail sketch of our endeavours, and more detailed literature is available for those who would care to read it. I have tried to avoid the temptation to comment out of 'our' experience to 'yours' in the hope that what I have written is so clearly stated that where the cap fits it might with grace be worn.

I consider the experiment to have been worth while, if difficult. We have proved our point that renewal in the local Church is both advisable and possible; and, further, that the influence of the Church is hoped and longed for by the greater majority of the community provided it can be seen that such work is relevant to our kind of society. The rewards of service outweigh the frustrations that crib and confine us. The former are worth having, the latter remain ever with us and must in the ultimate be dealt with, by local, district and national help and interest, if words, words, and more words are to lead to positive action.

# 3. Working Things Out

## THE ROCHDALE TEAM MINISTRY

A VITAL question for the Church in the twentieth century is 'What is a Team Ministry?' The difficulty lies in the fact that more and more team ministries are appearing on the Church scene, yet no set pattern of Team Ministry seems to emerge. For team ministries there is no easy classification. Like the chameleon, they change their colour to fit their circumstances.

One of the main problems facing any Team Ministry today is this fact that there are no real patterns which can be safely followed. All team ministries are different, all are formed in different situations, and all are formed in different ways. Therefore, although it is of value to write of a particular experiment in Team Ministry, there can be no easy formula for success and no general pattern to be followed and adopted in any situation. All team ministries are still in the early stages of working things out and it has at all times to be remembered that any desire for clarity and certainty has to be balanced against the need for enough flexibility to meet new and emerging circumstances.

In telling of the experiment based on the Champness Hall, Rochdale, some interesting pointers may be seen but from the start it must be said that what's suitable for Rochdale *cannot* be adequate anywhere else. Each church must work out its own salvation in the light of what the needs of the area served happen to be and taking into account the manpower and resources available.

### The Place

The Champness Hall stands very near the centre of Rochdale, one of the industrial towns of Lancashire. The Hall is the home of the Rochdale Methodist Mission, and it is a very large home. Unlike the average Methodist church, the Trust is almost self-supporting, as most of its income comes from letting various rooms and from the shops and office accommodation which form part of the Hall.

Morning services are still held in the main hall, with its three-manual pipe organ, tip-up seats (accommodating 1,500) and pleasantly decorated interior, but it is only full when used for outside lets (band concerts, school speech days, etc.), and then only rarely. The 120 adults and children who attend service on Sunday morning sit with rows of empty seats behind and above them (in the balcony). Evening services are now held for the most part in the Conference Room, on the first floor, where the old barn of a Sunday School room has been transformed into a modern suite of smaller rooms, offices, coffee lounge and prayer chapel.

On the second floor are the staff offices and the Youth Centre, with its badminton court, coffee bar, dance area, television lounge and other activity rooms. Part of the building has been converted into bed-sitting rooms, and at present there are eight residents in 'The Community'.

This, then, is the Champness Hall. It is the home of the Rochdale Methodist Mission, yet relatively few of the people who come through its doors each week are Methodists. Folk seeking National Health cards, immigrants needing help or advice, members of the youth club, girls coming to dancing classes, all these and many others come to the Champness Hall.

## The People

One of the most interesting things about the Rochdale Team Ministry is the variety of people it contains. At a later point I intend to discuss the implications of this, but for the moment it must suffice to enumerate the members and occupations of the team. In it there are male and female, ministerial and lay, young and less young.

First of all, there are the Staff of the Mission—Superintendent Minister, Deaconess, Warden and full-time Youth Leader. Then there are those engaged in what might nowadays be termed as 'Sector Ministries'—the North West Regional Lay Training Officer of the Methodist Church, teachers at various levels of the educational system, trainee social workers. Some members are single, others are married couples with children. Several members of the team actually live at the Hall, while others live in their own homes in different parts of Rochdale. There are members of the team who are following their chosen career, while the others are either training at the moment or are spending a while here before commencing their training.

An important fact to be borne in mind is that although there are those team members who have come to Rochdale by choice, there are those also who have been stationed here or whose work just happens to place them here for the duration of their present position. This means that the assumptions with which many team ministries are able to start do not operate in our particular case. Finding points of contact between those who have joined the team out of their own expressed wish to do so and those whose jobs make them automatically members of the team was one of the first essential tasks to be undertaken.

## The Work

One of the most hotly debated subjects in the Church today is the meaning of the word 'ministry'. Why do we call those whom the Church has ordained to the ministry of word and sacrament 'ministers', while Christians working in any other areas are called 'lay'? What has happened to the rest of Christ's ministries, such as the ministry of healing? Why is it that we tend to look upon ministers as those who have committed themselves to full-time Christian service, while a layman is one who does a 'secular' job and perhaps takes part in churchly activities in his spare time (and becomes a minister-substitute in the form of a Local Preacher or Society Steward)? Is it not true that the teacher is just as much a minister as the man who wears a clerical collar?

The debate still goes on. No answer seems to have been reached, and even if the answer has been found there is still a great gap between theory and practice. The Church still ordains some of its members but not all. The 'minister' is still the full-time churchman, who wears special clothes and does specially religious tasks. The 'layman' is still there to help the 'minister' if and when he has time to spare from his non-religious activity—his daily work.

A team ministry is a living witness to the fact that Christ's ministries cannot be limited in the way the Church has done over the past years. Although much of the work done by the team is similar to that which would be done by the traditional minister, there is a recognition that truly Christian activity is not just that done on church premises, or by a man paid as a full-time worker by the Church. The sphere of activity is widened to include the youth club, the technical college, the school, the hospital and other places of work.

Now, of course, there is nothing particularly new in Christians recognizing the social work and teaching professions as places where Christian ministry can be exercised. It would be interesting to see how a labourer or a skilled technician fitted his work into the team. We can claim no attempt or experiment in this field, and look eagerly to see what others have achieved. There are problems enough in trying to unite a group of a dozen or so people who work in similar fields, and in facing such problems our experience may well be of use to others.

How does the Rochdale Team operate? This question is one to which there is no easy answer. At times it seems that we'd be better going our own separate ways. At other times we see a vision —and that vision makes the team worthwhile. It would perhaps be clearest if I started by describing the things which we actually do together.

**Team Meetings**

Anyone who has belonged to a committee of any kind will know the problems which arise when it comes to fixing a date for the next meeting. Each committee member has his own external commitments, and it is very difficult to find a date which will be convenient to all concerned. This is certainly true in the case of the Rochdale Team Ministry. Each one of us is involved in all sorts of meetings, events and committees which make it hard to find times when we can all be together. We have therefore found it useful to decide upon a particular time of the month when we avoid other engagements, and the time decided upon was Sunday afternoon. The whole team come together over lunch and then the first half of the afternoon is spent in discussion. This gives us a period of three hours when we can be sure to be together each month (although even now it sometimes happens that one or other of us has another engagement which clashes but which must be fulfilled).

In addition to the monthly team meetings we occasionally take a Saturday off together in retreat. The trustees of a nearby country chapel have given us the use of their premises for this purpose.

Whether it be for three hours on a Sunday or six hours on a Saturday the meetings are important occasions. A chance is given to air grievances and to let off steam. If one member of the team has particular problems which he feels the other team members should know about, the meetings provide an opportunity to tell of the problem and discuss possible solutions. We have a chance to reflect on the nature of the team, the inter-relationship of its members, future possibilities, failures of the past and present. This may seem rather introspective in a time when the need is for out-ward-looking Christianity, but we have found it necessary to give at least a small amount of time to looking at ourselves and how we can better work together.

Team meetings provide the occasion for study, discussion, analysis and programming. We share our common concerns and we keep other members up to date on what is going on in our own sphere of operations. 'Fellowship' is perhaps not a good word to use in an age when it has come to be associated with tea parties at the manse, but if given something nearer its proper meaning, where we are talking in terms of building each other up (and if necessary knocking each other down first) in the setting of a com-munity then it could be said that we hold 'fellowship meetings'.

If one of us has an idea which might lead to a new extension of our Christian mission the team will look at the possibilities, examine the resources, try to foresee the pitfalls and then attempt to suggest a realistic course of action. Examples of this would in-clude suggestions of the youth leader (Mike) for a late night club for eighteens or twenty-fives, and the suggestion of the deaconess (Marjorie) that other people should be brought into visiting the sick and aged, the arrangements of courses run by members of the Chicago Ecumenical Institute, etc.

To think that all our time together is hard work would be wrong. Relaxing in each other's company is another way of deepening any working relationship. Whether it be singing folk songs, playing foot-ball on a deserted country road, chatting over coffee, or telling the latest joke heard in the youth club, our time of retreat is extremely valuable.

### In our Work and in our Play

Team meetings are the time when we all try to get together. For the most part, however, our contact with each other is in smaller group-ings. Each Wednesday those of us whose work entails a lot of time spent in the Hall hold a staff meeting followed by working day prayers. Even though we are probably only going through the programme of events during the coming week, staff meeting gives a chance to deal with any points that may crop up needing immed-iate action. It also provides Cyril with a source of admittedly reluctant volunteers if he wants any furniture moving in the Hall.

Quite often a couple of team members will be working together on a particular activity, and a system of mutual help operates. Dave assists Mike in the Youth Centre and also works with Marjorie in the junior club. Mike has made frequent visits to the Technical College in order to speak to one of Dave's classes. Several classes have also been brought to the Youth Centre to be shown round and to have a discussion in the coffee bar area (which is rather more friendly than the typical college classroom).

If one of the team is unable to take a scheduled meeting owing to illness or to another engagement then another team member will be there to fill the gap.

Team members who live in the Community chat together over evening coffee, and on many occasions other team members who happen to be in the building at that time will drop in to join them.

### Education and Caring

Our early team meetings were used to discuss the basic question of what we are doing and why we are doing it. Added to this was the further question of what this had to do with being a team ministry. Several team members produced working papers which helped formulate ideas which could then be discussed. At quite an early date the feeling was expressed that the team is a group of Christians trying together to find relevant forms of discipleship today, particularly in the areas of caring and education. These two areas of concern cannot be completely separated from each other and are often different aspects of the same activity.

In order to see what this means, let us have a brief look at the involvement of some team members as it works itself out during the week.

John Downes is engaged as the Superintendent Minister of Rochdale Methodist Mission. He is therefore involved in many of the administrative jobs known to every minister. At the same time he has sermons to prepare, meetings to chair, church newspaper to edit, not to mention the various other jobs which are the lot of a Methodist minister or the external events with which he is connected. His role can be seen as that of administrator but also as that of educator—he is trying to communicate (by written and spoken word) what he sees as relevant Christianity for today.

Marjorie James is in charge of most of the 'pastoral' duties. It is she who visits the sick, the aged, the problematic (although she is not alone in this visiting). Marjorie is also involved in the running of the various ladies' meetings of the Champness Hall, an Open Evening for Lonely People and two nights of junior youth club. Although this work would most easily fit into the 'caring' category, it can also be seen as education (particularly the youth club work).

Mike Twigg's youth work is definitely a mixture of caring and education. Young people from local schools, the technical college and places of work are able to come into the lunchtime club (held three days a week) or into the youth club itself (held four nights a week plus Sunday evening after church service). A lot of Mike's time is spent in counselling (caring) while the whole basis of youth club work is educational. He has also had considerable contact with the Technical College through going into some of Dave's classes. Teaching Liberal Studies in the College is so closely linked with youth work in general that it is difficult to say exactly where the one ends and the other begins.

Just a glance at the list of team members and their occupations will show how this twofold mission of caring and education works out in practice. But one may ask why caring and education? The answer to this is simple to find—in so far as the Christian mission must be seen as the task of trying to help people to achieve fullness of life and to make the most of their potential. Education helps man to develop and come to terms with the society in which he is placed. Caring looks after those who drop out or are inadequate, whether temporarily or permanently. The Rochdale Team sees its work as involvement in these areas of life—is this not what it means to 'do the things of Jesus today'?

**Saying and Doing**

There are team ministries which have been formed for an expressed purpose to answer the needs of a special area. This is not true of the Rochdale Team. We did not come into an area in which there was as yet no Christianity or in which Christianity was not already active. We are based on a church which already has quite a number of very active people within its membership. This means that any action which the team might want to take cannot be done solely on our own initiative. We are a group within an existing structure, rather than a completely isolated and self-sufficient body. If we have, for example, new ideas for forms of worship, these ideas are passed on to the Worship Commission of the Church or to the Leaders' Meeting. When a special need arises or a special task is to be undertaken it is not the team ministry, but an action group formed by church members which tackles the problem. Mention has already been made of the Worship Commission. Other groups have recently been started which hope to deal with questions such as Education, World Hunger, Unattached Youth, Tensions within the Church, etc.

One may well ask, then, why bother with a team at all? If it is not some form of action group what is it for? These are valid questions. It has already been suggested that there is a way in which the team is a glorified house group, met for study and analysis, rather than an action-orientated body. When there are already workers in any field in which we are interested it would be a waste of resources to overlap on what is going on in the existing situation. It is far better to help in making the most of what resources there are than to try to compete in order to expand our own empire.

This is not to say that we are all talk and no action. We do not boast of a great deal of common activity, but what we do in our own areas is seen in a different context when discussed as team matters. Mike is not left in isolation to do the best he can in his youth work. What he does is seen in the context of the group. To his own training and experience are added insights from other spheres of operation—teaching, social work, etc. And this is true for what each team member does. So, the team is an attempt to increase individual efficiency by adding to the resources of each member the resources of the group.

## Team and Congregation

It is often said that the average church member neglects his Christian duty on the grounds that such work can and should be left to the minister—after all, he's paid to do it. So we get a situation of overworked clergy and underworked laymen. What effect does the presence of a team ministry have on this?

It must be remembered that the Rochdale Team Ministry consists of 'immigrants'—people who have come into the town. It is therefore not completely surprising that there is sometimes a feeling of suspicion on the part of the natives of Rochdale. Champness Hall is 'their church'. If a team member doesn't like the arrangement or gets himself in a mess of any sort he can easily go away to fresh pastures. Rochdale isn't his home town. His only link with the place is the team ministry. His loyalties are not the same as those of the Rochdaleian.

Added to this is the problem that a team ministry is not a recognized institution in the structure of the Methodist Church. It is not a democratic body. The Methodist Society at Champness Hall do not 'elect' members to the Team. So, if it appears that the Team is making decisions which should rightly be made by, for example, the Leaders' Meeting, there is some disquiet. The 'us' versus 'them' barrier can easily arise. And it is not simply a question of team members trying to communicate to the church members what they are trying to do. By including laymen in the team we are saying that the Church's ministry is not to be undertaken solely by those who have been ordained by the Church. But we are saying more than that. The Church is that body of people who are 'doing the things of Jesus' today. As such it can obviously not be limited simply to members of the team ministry. The team is a group of people who try to see their task in terms of corporateness rather than individuality, but the task itself is the same task as that in which all other church members are involved.

Recently this point has been discussed a great deal by various groups in the Rochdale Mission. The team itself has been somewhat worried about the danger of isolation. The Local Preachers' Meeting has been interested in how it's members fit into the picture. This discussion is ongoing. All that can be said at the moment is that there is definitely a growing recognition that the titles of 'minister' or 'team ministry member' do not denote a position higher up the religious scale than that of 'ordinary church member'. The team is a useful working group. It is a group which provides sustenance for its members, and can be described as 'therapeutic'. The team can be compared to a house group or fellowship group— a group who come together and talk things out, feeling that if they see things corporately the things can be done better than if they were only on the individual level. Decision making (thus usurping the power of established Church structures) is not the job of the team.

## Outworkings

The team ministry recognizes the importance of groups other than those traditionally associated with the Church. Often a person who is in fact fast becoming disillusioned with the Church will be willing to join a lively group so long as it is not too strongly linked with the Establishment. In Tony Wesson's Lay Training Project this fact is becoming abundantly clear, but it can also be seen at work in the 'Ashram'. This is a group of youngish people, mainly from the North of England (although some come from greater distances) who meet at quarterly intervals to discuss radical Christian thought and to see what action this thought necessitates. Here is not the place to go into a detailed history of Ashram and its achievements. One event, however, is of importance.

At the residential Ashram held at the end of November, 1968, the idea came into being of a community house in the multi-racial area of Rochdale—Tweedale Street. Why the idea arose is difficult to pinpoint, but it seems a natural outcome of the thought about Christian community living and the need for a Christian presence in potential problem areas—thought which had been expressed at previous Ashrams. In November several Ashram members formed the nucleus of what is called the 'Committee of Forty'. Each 'member' of the 'Committee' promised to pay £25 towards the purchase of a house in Tweedale Street. The money is now coming in and it is hoped to buy the house some time this year. Its occupants will be for the early stages two present members of the team (Gladys Brierley and Chris Blackwell) plus another volunteer, who will be invited to join the team.

Quite what the community house will achieve is as yet difficult to say. It can be said for sure, however, that it will be an experiment in the realm of community living (as a Christian activity). Otherwise, it will be very much a case of Tweedale Street 'writing the agenda'. The occupants of the house will have their normal jobs to go to during the day, but will be at home in the evenings. The house may well be an 'open house' so that anyone in the area who has problems can drop in for a chat. Rooms may be made available for the use of people living nearby (providing the base for community activities). It is likely that one room will be converted into a chapel. Social service agencies will be invited to use the house as an outpost. This will enable them to have a local base for counselling sessions and will give them an opportunity to have someone on hand who can give help and advice to those who require it.

Some members of Ashram have offered to live in the house for short periods to run particular projects. For example, a married couple might live in for a fortnight of their holiday period. In that time they could organize a survey, run a children's playgroup, or tackle anything else that was needed on a short term basis.

The community house is for us a completely new field of operation, so it will be interesting to see just what does develop.

## The Future

It is hoped that this outline of the Rochdale Team Ministry, although brief, has been enough to show the sort of doing and thinking that is going on here. From the outset it was stated that no experiment of this kind can really ever be called complete and successful. If we did think that we had succeeded or had brought things to a happy conclusion then obviously it would not be long before we became stagnant. We live in a world of constant tensions and demands, and it is this world that we are trying to serve. New tensions and new demands in our work are therefore to be continually expected.

What, then, of the future? It is impossible to say what the future might hold. By 1970 we will have lost some team members and gained new ones. The new arrivals will presumably bring with them their own ideas and experiences—so the team will develop and change. This is a good and necessary thing, not to be feared or bemoaned. Our experiment will go on. So will experiments elsewhere. Experiments are needed today, and perhaps what we have tried may encourage others to see what they can do. Who knows what will happen over the years to come?

The experimenters of this world are never able to sit back and think their work is over. They must constantly search for what is new. Security is not for them. But the Christian faith through the ages has never offered security in normally accepted human terms. We are all called to take the leap of faith, knowing only that the Lord Christ goes before us.

[*The Team Ministry at Rochdale came into existence through the initiative of the then Superintendent Minister, the Revd Dr John Vincent.*]

# 4. 'New Christian—New Age' Programme

## AT MARPLE METHODIST CHURCH

### The test bed

MARPLE is typical of many small dormitory towns which serve large cities and conurbations. Its present population is about 21,000, although the increase over the past decade has been rapid and is expected to continue. It is situated on the Cheshire border, about twelve miles south-east of Manchester, and five miles from Stockport, the nearest large town. Marple is a mainly middle-class place with a Liberal majority on the Council and it is justly conscious and proud of its historic and scenic values. There is not much overt social life in the town, but a multitude of clubs, catering for the most esoteric interests, flourish in homes and church halls. It is a pleasant place to live in and it is often difficult to realize that this self-contained green belt community is only a dozen miles from one of our largest cities.

The population of Marple includes a high percentage of young marrieds, for it attracts many aspiring managerial and professional workers who are transferred to Manchester and who can get a mortgage on a Wimpey house. Consequently the birth rate is high, there are a lot of young children and the schools (and the Sunday Schools) are full to overflowing. But it is a mobile population and for many of its families Marple is but one of a number of stepping stones in the career pattern. Churches perhaps are the most affected of all the institutions in Marple by this rapid turnover of population—and there are a lot of them to be affected. Within the boundaries of the Urban District are five Anglican Churches, five Methodist churches, two Congregational, two Roman Catholic, one Friends' Meeting House, one Christian Science Church and one meeting of the Independent Evangelical Alliance—almost one

Church for every thousand people. Fortunately there is in Marple a strong tradition of ecumenical involvement, and the local Council of Churches is a very effective force in planning and co-ordinating the activities of its member Churches.

The Methodist Church involved in the 'New Christian—New Age' experiment is the largest of the five Methodist churches. It has a stable membership of just over 300, a very strong Junior Church (300 children) and most of the groups and societies that are traditionally associated with a Methodist church of this size. Some of the things it has done have been good and successful and others have not. The church has never had a particular local mission and, despite its size, financial solvency has been a continuing problem in recent years. About four years ago, following the sale and demolition of a neighbouring Methodist church, the premises were extended by the addition of a magnificent wing to the buildings, containing a spacious concourse, and several large rooms. The present buildings are large, extensively modernized and more than adequate for the internal needs of the society.

The members of the church have, no doubt, always been aware of the discrepancy between the actual corporate life of the society and the potential effect which it could have on the community if it took seriously the claims of Jesus. But it is not too difficult to come to terms with this kind of awareness. Of course, it is good for a church to care for its own members in all sorts of ways and, of course, the Christian gospel was being preached in Marple by the corporate and individual witness of its members. Of course, there is a limit to the amount of time that busy people can give to church affairs—and the amount of money they can give. Of course, it is unreasonable to expect people of different ages and backgrounds to share a common view of the mission of the Church. Of course, it is often difficult to translate the words of Jesus to our modern situation. Of course . . . a thousand times.

Three years ago the Leaders' Meeting decided that the time had come to move from rationalizations to corporate commitment and the experiment of the 'New Christian—New Age' programme was conceived. What follows is a description of what the experiment is trying to do, how it is set up and operated and what it has achieved. It is still going on, and it may be several years before the full effects of it can be evaluated, but even at this early stage an attempt at an honest appraisal is a useful exercise.

**What we are trying to do**

Our starting point was the assumption, not that the church was in a state of hopeless spiritual and social decay, but that it was lacking in fresh ideas, in new ways of capturing the tremendous reservoir of talent that existed among its membership and in its impact on the community. The traditional pattern of Church organization was, for our church at least, failing to provide an adequate framework within which we could examine the meaning of Christianity in the 1960s and translate it into the actual concrete situations of our social life. If somebody joined the church and wanted to do something, we could have offered him the Choir, or the Sunday School, or helping with the Youth Club ... and that was about it. The mechanisms did not exist for getting him involved in community service, or in planning the worship of the church, or in pastoral visiting, or in house fellowships, or in national and international affairs, in the arts, in Christian education, or in a thousand other things that ought to be the deliberate concern of the Church today. As a family we had scarcely disciplined ourselves to ensure that these things were our regular business.

The title 'New Christian—New Age' was intended to reflect this underlying aim of trying new methods and new approaches in our task of being Christians in Marple in the 1960s. What was conceived was nothing less than a comprehensive programme of renewal and outreach, integrating all the main sections of the church's life under one theme. The introductory booklet described the programme in this way:

It is a co-ordinated programme of worship, service, culture and education that tries to put the contemporary Christian Church in a position of lively and intelligent leadership in the community. It is founded on the belief that Christ's people should have an informed and compassionate interest in what is happening in God's world, and should be prominent among those who are trying to bring about social and moral change. It is founded on the belief that what happens *in* the Church, in our worship and fellowship and recreation, and what happens *outside* the Church, in our witness and service and concern, are equal parts of our corporate life as Christians. We believe that it is our job as Christians to use our gifts of time and talents and money in a responsible way to enhance our worship, to sensitize ourselves to the needs of others, and to educate ourselves in the gracious and beautiful things of life.

The stated objectives were to give direction and unity to the life and work of the church; to present the Christian faith in modern terms; and to activate the discipleship of a greater number of church members. And at the heart of the programme was the notion of the church as a family, knowing and caring for each other, and mutually supporting each other in the various and diverse roles that each was playing.

### How the programme was organized

Both 1967 and 1968 were years of initial exploration and experiment and it is difficult in retrospect to recall exactly what was done in each year. For the reader this is of no consequence, for the broad outline of the programme was the same for each year. In describing how it was organized, however, some chronological errors may have been made in this description, and for this apologies are made.

Certain aspects of the existing situation had to be considered in devising the organization of the 'New Christian—New Age' programme. One was that many of the groups within the church were already fulfilling vitally important tasks and could not be radically disturbed. Among these are the Junior Church and the Youth Club. Another consideration was that, although some of the other groups could have usefully lost their identities in a completely new framework, there are practical limits to the amount of change and innovation that can be introduced in a short time. Thirdly, the co-operative links that existed between the church and the Council of Churches had to be preserved. And finally, the scheme had to link in with the traditional constitution of the church and the regular pattern of government through the Leaders' Meeting.

The programme revolves around a series of seven commissions, each of which is responsible for a major area of the church's life: worship, fellowship, national and international affairs, publicity, the arts, outreach and service, and pastoral care. Each Commission has a Director, who is responsible to the Leaders' Meeting for the work of his Commission, and a group of ex-officio members who form the basis of the Commission at the start of each year. Thus, for example, the 'constitution' of the Commission on Worship states that the permanent members of that Commission consist of the Minister, a Society Steward, a Poor Steward, a choir representative, a local preacher and representatives of the Junior Church and the Youth Club. This group of permanent members is then expanded by the addition of those who, for that year, want to base their discipleship in the work of this particular Commission. The underlying aim of this approach is to have each member of the church making a specific and organized contribution to one aspect of the work of the church, rather than, as happened before, a diffuse and uneconomical gesture of sympathy towards a number of different groups. Ideally, members join just one Commission each year, so that the whole scheme is an effective way of getting busy people working together in an economical and efficient fashion.

In addition to the permanent membership, a series of jobs are laid down in the 'constitution' of each Commission. Thus, for example, the jobs of the Arts Commission are to educate the church in the role of the visual, dramatic and musical arts in worship and in recreation; to encourage and organize the church's use of them; and to co-ordinate the cultural and social activities of the various organizations in the church. The specified jobs for each Commission are, of course, flexible, and they can and do change from year to year. The purpose of them is partly to provide a basis on which each Commission can plan its work for the year, and partly to continually remind the members of the Commission of the church's obligations in that area of life.

The Directors of each Commission are appointed to the Leaders' Meeting, and it is this Meeting that evaluates the progress of the scheme and recommends alterations in it. It also retains responsibility for co-ordinating the activities of the church with those of the local Council of Churches, and with Circuit and District policies. The purpose of the 'New Christian—New Age' programme is not to usurp the authority of the Leaders' Meeting, but rather to enable it to function more effectively than it had hitherto done. By the middle of the second year of the programme there were signs that this purpose was being achieved; the greater part of our Leaders' Meeting was spent in a discussion of the nature of the Church in the 1970s, and a consideration of possible areas of radical change in the second half of the twentieth century. The programme had provided the stimulus for this kind of discussion to be seen as a part of the task of the church leaders.

## The Commissions

1 *Worship* It is gratifying, in terms of priorities, that in the first two years of the programme the Worship Commission was probably the most active and successful of all, and some notable

achievements can be recorded even at this early stage. The greatest achievement is probably that it has set many worshippers thinking constructively and often critically about the innovations that it has introduced. Many of the new ideas have met with opposition, but it is well recognized that conflict plays a central part in change and development.

The Worship Commission meets regularly to plan the worshipping life of the church, and its work has developed in four main areas. First, it has established a pattern of monthly themes and weekly subjects that provide cohesion to the whole programme. (This pattern has lent itself well to the Faith, Work and Worship syllabus in 1968/69.) Secondly, it has instituted a series of set orders of worship for the morning family services, which are specifically designed to enable the Junior Church scholars to have a much closer interest in the first part of the service before they leave. The orders include a modern statement of the Creed, simple prayers that express the basic faith of Christianity, and the appointed lesson of the day in the Junior Church syllabus. Thirdly, a Commissioning Service has been introduced at the beginning of each year of the programme (in the Autumn), which replaces the various dedication services for Class Leaders, Sunday School teachers and so on. And fourthly, the Commission has experimented widely with 'workshop' services, in which new techniques are used to fulfil the traditional purposes of worship. On Industrial Sunday, for example, the church was used for a display of the various tools that people use in their jobs, and the evening sermon was replaced by a discussion between representatives of a trade union and a company management. In another service, a psychologist answered questions from parents about family problems; in another a totally disabled woman spoke of what life is like when perpetually confined to a wheelchair. At Christmas, the Moravian service of the Christingle is enacted; at Whitsun a series of folk songs formed the basis of our celebration of the Holy Spirit in the world; on Remembrance Sunday an ecumenical service was fashioned on the theme of the Universal Declaration of Human Rights, and a pacifist was cross-examined about his beliefs. Music, drama, discussions, films, interviews, displays—these are but some of the ways through which we have tried to reach a Christian perspective on world poverty, education, the homeless, racism, sex, industrial relations, parenthood and the family, war and peace, human rights, and a host of other topics.

The Worship Commission, more perhaps than any other, has

typified the spirit of experimentation and innovation that is at the heart of the programme. It has not always succeeded in its ventures, but it has drawn together people of diverse interests and opinions into a common concern for the worshipping life of the church.

2 *Fellowship* The broad aim of the Commission is to create situations in which the church can, in the nature of a family, meet together in small and large groups to talk, to share problems, experiences and friendship, and to learn. Although the 'constitution' of the Commission charges it to consider a number of means of fellowship, two main approaches have been used in the first two years.

The first approach is through the concept of house groups—not a new idea, certainly, but one that had not been extensively tried at this church in recent years. It was hoped in the first year that the groups would capitalize on the momentum of the 'People Next Door' campaign, which had been extremely well organized in Marple, and in the second year that they would link up with similar house meetings of the neighbouring Anglican and Congregational Churches. Neither of these hopes were fully realized (although the Council of Churches has made the establishment of a comprehensive ecumenical house group system, the number one objective in its programme for the coming year). As a rule, however, the regular group members were in any case centrally involved in the church, and the groups represented a means of fellowship for a very small proportion of the church members.

The second approach is through monthly group meetings for the entire family of the church. The Commission was soon conscious of the fact that the house fellowships tended to be homogeneous in composition, and that they did not provide a means for people to get to know others with whom, in the normal course of things, they might do no more than pass the time of day. To emphasize the 'togetherness' of the monthly meetings (which are called 'Focus' meetings), all the church organizations that normally have weekday meetings cancel their programmes on Focus week. The pattern of the Focus meeting is varied, but the most common format is to have a talk from the guest speaker, then to divide into groups to consider points or questions which have been raised in the talk, and then to come together again for a general discussion, with the speaker answering questions and clarifying points of difficulty. The Focus meetings are given maximum publicity and, as far as possible, the guest speakers are distinguished and eminent people. The subjects of the Focus meetings tie in with the theme for the month, and have been on such topical issues as the challenge of science, drug addiction, Biafra, Czechoslovakia, homelessness, monasticism, immigration, student unrest and mental health. The most provocative of the lot was an impassioned dialogue between a team of 'Marxist' students and our members.

3 *National and International* With so much concern about the Church's role in Marple, it is very easy to become defeatingly parochial in outlook. The Commission on National and International affairs exists to force the church's attention from time to time beyond the boundaries of the parish to the wider issues facing the nation and the world. The task of this Commission is thus a difficult one, for although the church has for a long time been a regular contributor to Home and Overseas Missions, to Oxfam, Christian Aid, and so on, it has probably largely ceased to think or pray constructively about the projects to which it contributes. It is a peculiarly difficult job to get people in conscious recognition of what has for long been a subconscious familiarity.

The Commission has, in the first two years, chosen a sensible and realistic line of approach, namely, to work through the Council of Churches, and to stimulate our involvement in the Council's international work. A number of projects have been successfully completed in this way, and it is likely that as a result of this approach (and entirely as a by-product of the Commission's work) a greater proportion of members than ever before have learnt about the Council of Churches and what it is doing. One project involved a Saturday morning protest in Marple High Street about the political oppression in Rhodesia and was accompanied by a sign-in in the local park. Another project involved the use of the church premises, during the Week of Prayer for Christian Unity, for a very large and impressive exhibition of ecumenical achievement throughout the world. A third job of the Commission has been to represent the church's interest in the scheme, proposed by the Council of Churches and sponsored by the Urban District Council, of linking Marple with a 'twin' town—Monkon Bamenda in the West Cameroons.

The potential area of work of the National and International Commission is vast, and the projects described above represent but a small part of the Commission's charge. Among the projects that it is hoped to start in subsequent years is one to organize the church's hospitality to visitors from abroad (especially students), and another to establish a Christian Aid shop in Marple. But this Commission has suffered from a lack of support, and it seems after two years that still new approaches must be tried in interesting people in its work.

4 *Publicity* An effective church is an articulate church that can communicate clearly both to its own members and to those outside. Publicity is seen as a skilled and creative job that is entirely worthy of its own Commission. The jobs listed in the 'Constitution' of the Commission are: to provide display and publicity material as requested; to produce a monthly newsletter; to operate a Press bureau; to be responsible for all notice-boards; to maintain a current affairs board in the concourse; to participate in the Council of Church's Ecumenical Newsletter; and to keep the church informed of progress in the 'New Christian—New Age' programme.

Of these, three jobs have been singled out for special attention in the first two years. The first arose from the primary need to inform people about the 'New Christian—New Age' programme, about how it was to be organized, and about their part in it. For this purpose, the Commission produced a ten-page booklet which was distributed to every family connected with the church—700 in all. The booklet first explained the purpose and rationale of the programme, and then described the constitution of each Commission, including the jobs that they were charged to do, and the names and addresses of the Directors. Finally, a tear-off questionnaire was appended on which people could indicate which Commission (and which specific project) they wanted to be associated with.

The second main occupation of the Publicity Commission has been with the production of a printed monthly newsletter designed to centre on the theme of the month. The format of the newsletter changes from year to year (there have so far been two editors in two years!) but it is essentially a simple document, conveying a small amount of important material, in an atractive and eye-catching design. It is circulated through a team of distributors, and reaches about 700 families each month. On a larger scale, the third major concern of this Commission has been with the Council of Church's Ecumenical Newsletter 'New Dimension', which is an altogether larger and glossier production, and which is delivered free to *every* household in Marple. Two editions have so far been produced, but it is still too early to assess the value of this project.

The Publicity Commission requires two very scarce commodities in order to work effectively—talent and money. Good publicity involves genuine skills of design and draughtsmanship, and it is not cheap. Neither commodity is abundant in Marple, although the artistic skills of some Youth Club members have been harnessed to the work of the Commission, and the Leaders' Meeting have allocated a monthly sum to a publicity account. But until the skills and the cash are in greater supply the work of this Commission will necessarily be limited—although it offers magnificent scope for the ingenious, the persuasive and the improvisers.

5 *Arts* 'It is', says the 'New Christian—New Age' booklet, 'as proper to praise the Lord on a twelve-string guitar and in modern dramatic form as by hymn-singing and organ-playing'. The jobs assigned to this Commission have already been described, and the Commission has distinguished itself with the amount and quality of the projects produced under its aegis. From the choir have come superb performances of Haydn's 'Creation' and Handel's 'Messiah', as well as many musical services of various kinds. From the Youth Club have come the pop music and folk song of some of the services, and two modern dramatic representations—'Show us a King' and 'A Man Dies'. From the Sunday School have come hilarious pantomimes. From outside the church have come orchestras and choirs of a very high standard. Perhaps the only major area in which the Arts Commission has not yet excelled is the visual arts—and that is their challenge for future years.

In many ways, of course, the job of the Arts Commission has been the easiest of all. Methodism was indeed born in song, and the contemporary Methodist finds it easier and more congenial to sing than to feed the hungry and clothe the naked. Nevertheless, this group has achieved its success by imaginative planning and efficient organization.

6 *Outreach and Service* For the same reasons that the Arts Commission has much in its favour, so this Commission has much against it. In so far as the Church is characterized by its concern for and service in the community, this Commission is one of the most important, yet in this church (as in so many others) the record of service to the community was limited. The hesitation of many Christians to indulge in unselfconscious evangelism or to identify with the poor and underprivileged is not something that can be changed through administrative or organizational engineering.

In many ways, therefore, this group was the least successful, and it attracted the discipleship of very few members—by the second year only 3 per cent of all the members of the church were associated with this Commission. As with the National and International Commission, much of the work of this group was done in conjunction with the Council of Churches and its Service Committee, especially in terms of 'outreach'. During the first two years of the programme, no unilateral projects were started with a specifically evangelical aim, although there is much scope for this kind of work in Marple, especially in visiting new housing estates. The thrust of the Commission's work was centred around four main concerns. First, some long-overdue links were forged with a local authority residential home in Marple for mothers and children who run into difficulties in family and household management, and who are usually referred by the Courts. The home relies heavily on voluntary help of all kinds, and the Churches have a particularly valuable role in helping to provide a background and example of family stability to these unstable and insecure mothers. By the end of the second year of the programme, one member was giving weekly cookery lessons at the home, another was helping with the routine tasks of sewing and mending. Others were inviting the children and/or the mothers for tea and Junior Church staff had taken groups of children on various outings. Secondly, the young people of the church were running a weekly youth club, at the local Mencaps centre for mentally handicapped teenagers drawn from a very wide catchment area. It is, in fact, inaccurate to claim this piece of service as one of the Commission's projects, as the Youth Club had been associated with Mencaps in this way before the 'New Christian—New Age' programme ever started. It is interesting to note that in doing this the Youth Club were representing the church's only 'formal' service link with the community. Thirdly, the Commission has begun a 'Car Ferry Service'. The idea originally started as a service to the elderly members of the church, to ensure that there was always somebody available to transport them for worship, but it quickly became apparent that a rota of this nature has much wider possibilities. Within the church, the demand for transport is often as high on weekdays as on Sundays, and the joy of housebound people in having car rides on summer weekends can easily be overlooked. Within the community, a host of uses can easily be found for the regular availability of cars, and it is planned that these will be gradually explored by the Commission. The fourth main area of action has been in providing regular visiting and an emergency aid service for elderly people. Again, this originated as a service to the church members, but the possibility of extending it to the whole community is an exciting one. One of the long-term projects of the Council of Churches is to implement a 'Fish' scheme, based on the one started in the Oxford Diocese, and it is hoped that our church will have much to contribute to the project, both in terms of personnel and of experience in running a scheme of this type.

The Commission has, in addition to these major activities, tackled several smaller jobs, such as the organization of carol singing parties at Christmas, and the custodianship of equipment for handicapped people. For the future, the Commission is hoping to launch a campaign, in collaboration with the Child Poverty Action Group, to educate people in the welfare benefits to which they are entitled.

7 *Community Groups* The aim of this Commission is to rejuvenate the pastoral work of the church, and to shift some of the responsibility for it from the minister to the members. Lay visiting can easily cease when the distribution of the class tickets becomes a matter of just putting them through the letter box, yet the involvement of members in the task of pastoral care is an essential part of a caring Church.

Marple was first divided in forty small areas, and a community leader was appointed for each area. An area contains, on average, eight members of the church and almost twenty families who have some connection with the church (such as having children in the Junior Church). The aim of the scheme is for the leaders to be in regular social contact with the members and 'adherents' of their areas, and in this way to be alert to any problems or needs which they may have, and in which the church, directly or indirectly, can offer help. It is, in fact, a local adaptation of a widely adopted 'early warning' system, and although in this case it is intended primarily as a means of discharging pastoral responsibility towards our own families in the church, it can easily be extended to include, for example, new families moving into Marple. The advantages of the system are partly in involving more people in lay visiting, and partly in enabling the minister to make a more economical use of his time.

The community leaders are responsible for keeping up-to-date records of all with whom they are in social contact, and they meet regularly for half-an-hour before each quarterly Leaders' Meeting. They have two specific jobs. The first is to distribute the 'New Christian—New Age' newsletter each month to all the families on their lists, and this should always involve a personal contact with each family. This is also the principle underlying the distribution of class tickets, but there are probably some advantages in having small geographical areas as the units of the system, for the community leader is then much more likely to see his 'members' regularly in the course of daily life. The second specific task of the community leaders is to operate the pastoral table and the visitors' book in the church concourse. The visitors' book is self-explanatory: it serves the dual purpose of stimulating a sense of affinity with the church among 'out of town' visitors, and of recording the addresses of Marple visitors for later follow-ups. The 'pastoral table' is a simple post-box for notes or memoranda from or about people who would like to see the minister. At the beginning of the programme each family had a few copies of a printed postcard requesting a visit, and stating briefly the reason for the request; and the community leaders had separate cards to fill in for any of their contacts whom they felt to be in any kind of need. The table is emptied regularly, and the minister is in this way kept in regular touch with those who most need his attention.

## What has it all achieved?

The 'New Christian—New Age' programme was designed as a comprehensive plan for modern discipleship. It is essentially an attempt at getting a church to accept the responsibilities and obligations that Jesus has put upon it, but it is an *organized* attempt. Our previous experience had been that the 'traditional' ways of running a church were not particularly effective, and that a completely new approach was needed to provide fresh ideas, to challenge accepted and reactionary practices, and to provoke *all* the members of the church into examining seriously the claims that Christ has on their lives. What the programme does is to start with the existing social patterning of groups and responsibilities, and to cut across them and reconstitute them on totally different criteria. Whereas before the natural social groupings had been roughly in terms of age/sex/social class homogeneity, after the introduction of the programme they were much more in terms of *function* (centring on the Commissions) with each functional group containing a wide diversity of social characteristics.

But how has it all worked out in practice? In re-reading what has been written above about the work of the Commissions, the writers are struck by the considerable discrepancy between the theoretical formulation of the programme (the ideal type) and the way it has actually worked in practice. The descriptions of the Commissions are, for obvious reasons, as favourable as possible, and although all the projects described have been actually completed or started, the quality of some of them is very much lower than the descriptions might suggest. Overall, there is considerable disappointment at the relative failure of the programme to yield the hoped-for response. The point has already been made that two years is too short a time to permit a substantial evaluation, but even at this stage some items of the balance-sheet can be sketched in.

On the credit side, the programme has provided a series of specific and finite targets, which are always easier to work towards than diffuse and generalized goals (such as 'spreading the gospel'). There has been an honest attempt to translate the gospel into the actual and concrete terms of Marple in our decade, and the mere description of the programme provides a visible and logical over-view of the Church's mission in terms that are understandable to all its members. Even if they have not responded, it can at least be said that each member has been confronted with a challenging interpretation of what it means to belong to a Christian community today, and that itself is no mean achievement. But more tangible successes can be noted. Lay participation has undoubtedly temporarily increased in many areas of the church's life, though not always in those where one would wish to see the greatest increase. The work of the Worship Commission is a good example of the way in which the concept of the programme has involved many more people in active participation in shaping the life of the church than could ever have been achieved before. Moreover, many of the projects have been substantially successful when, without the programme, it is doubtful whether they would even have been considered. The fact that many of the projects have met with an abortive fate and have led to a concomitant degree of disappointment cannot conceal the fact that many more of the projects and tasks have substantially achieved their aims.

Statistical criteria of performance in a programme of this nature are notoriously elusive, and we would not attach much weight to them. For the record, however, it may be noted that although the membership figures have remained stable for the two years, the attendances at family worship on Sunday mornings have increased, and it is not unusual for the church to be full for the first part of the service. More important, however, than these statistical criteria is the feeling that the society has grown together as a family. The cliques still exist, of course, but the programme has encouraged much more social and spiritual intercourse between different kinds of people, and has fostered a stronger 'we-feeling'. The innovation of an annual Anniversary Dinner is but one manifestation of a deeper sense of family responsibility that seems to have grown out of the programme.

These are all substantial achievements that justify the innovation and continued existence of the 'New Christian—New Age' programme at Marple. But there is a debit side—or, more accurately, a limitation to the credit that can be attached to the programme. The disappointingly poor response of the church is another manifestation of the basic fact about these kinds of schemes—that one cannot change people's motives and behaviour *just* by juggling with the organizational framework. For a while a new scheme attracts support and interest (new things always do), but after a while the former apathies set in. In Marple the signs of this were clear enough. The 'image' of the 'New Christian—New Age' programme has probably never had very much impact on the majority of members, and only a small minority have really identified with it in a personal way. It has never been inextricably bound up with the very existence of the church in the way that, for example, a full stewardship campaign usually is. This may be the fault of publicity and of the failure to exploit known techniques of stimulating a sense of involvement and commitment: more probably it reflects the fact that people have limits to the sacrifice which they are prepared to make in their Christian commitment, and that a programme of this nature will not alter the range of these limits very much. It is instructive, for example, that more people have become involved in the Worship Commission than in the Service or Fellowship Commissions. By the end of the second year of the programme the majority of those who were still centrally involved in it were the ones who would have been at the heart of things in any case—regardless of what kind of organization was used. At the start of this year the response to the tear-off questionnaire at the end of the information booklet was about 15 per cent, and this one fact perhaps best illustrates the failure of the programme to have any widespread impact on the church. The impact in the community was even less, although this was the one area where one desperately hoped to see the greatest strides being made. Much of the church's service to the community is made through the Council of Churches (and whilst this is not intended to be deprecatory, it cannot be claimed as a success of the programme), and apart from this the record is flimsy. Above all, the introduction of the programme did not make it appreciably easier to get 'fringe' members, in any numbers, involved in appropriate activities: it merely increased and specified the range of tasks for which workers had to be found.

Finally, a few general comments can be made about the 'New Christian—New Age' programme which help to set our successes and failures in perspective, and which may be relevant to others who plan similar schemes. There is first the question of how completely innovatory a scheme of this type can be. Ideally, we feel that the Commissions should replace almost all of the existing groups in the church, with the exception of certain obvious and key organizations, together with a radical restructuring of our church organization. It is only in this way that members can become fully committed to the new framework. In fact, as we have found, there is a limit to the amount of change that can be introduced at once and at Marple the programme in the first two years has been running alongside the full range of usual activities. The programme is sufficiently flexible to allow this, with a gradual phasing-out of other groups occurring as commitment to the programme grows, but the fact that 'New Christian—New Age' had almost to compete with other activities for support undoubtedly detracted substantially from the impact it could make.

Next, the question of personalities and leadership is important. In Marple, the programme was much more the brainchild of one man—The Minister—than this description has implied. The original idea, the detailed development of the organization and the leadership in implementing the programme all derive predominantly from him, and after two years it is doubtful whether 'New Christian—New Age' could have a viable existence without him. At this point in time, and with no prescience of the future, it seems unlikely that it will survive his departure at the appointed time. A handful of members have understood the significance and the potential of the programme, and they have provided genuine leadership at the centre of things, but they would probably not be able to keep the scheme alive when a new minister takes over. To be a long-term proposition, emotional commitment must be spread quite widely, and this should probably have been deliberately attempted as an integral self-perpetuating part of the programme.

Lastly, the programme has the obvious merit of incurring no additional costs, but the disadvantage that it does not specifically embrace money-raising activities in the way that a stewardship campaign does. It can, however, be easily integrated with such a campaign, and in fact at the end of the first year in Marple a motion was raised at the Leaders' Meeting that the church should undertake one. The motion was rejected on the ostensible grounds that the Meeting preferred to continue experimenting with 'New Christian—New Age'; but the rejection was a major disappointment to some members who felt that a stewardship campaign would provide just the kind of motivational stimulus that was lacking in the programme, and that might give it the chance of a long-term existence.

In summary, 'New Christian—New Age' has been an interesting and worthwhile experiment that has achieved much in individual projects, but that overall has met with patchy and inconsistent success. Our experience to date suggests that this kind of programme does not hold the answer to the dwindling membership figures or the increasingly vociferous charge that the Church is irrelevant in modern society: and we believe that this is because it is not radical enough. 'New Christian—New Age' tinkers with the carburettor adjustment at a time when the big ends have gone. Perhaps nothing short of a new engine can save the Church from the scrap-heap. But that is another book!

# 5. The South Abingdon Venture

ABINGDON-ON-THAMES is divided in two, not by the Thames itself but by one of its smaller tributaries, the Ock. Until the last fifty years or so the town developed round its centre North of the Ock and was, in common with most market towns, a collection of shops, public houses, churches and dwellings. With the growing industrialization of the South Midlands between the wars, Abingdon expanded, with estates being built both North and South of the River Ock. More recently, large housing estates have been built in central and northern areas by the Atomic Energy Authority. At present the estate South of the Ock is being considerably enlarged by both Council and private developers. However, so far, it has few amenities and no church.

In the Autumn of 1966 the deacons of the Abingdon Congregational Church, appreciating this lack of amenities, and realizing that their own church building was under-utilized suggested the following plan. Although their own church building occupies a central position in the Town Square it is old, unpretentious and needing many repairs and the deacons felt that with a membership of about forty it would be better to sell or lease the present site and use the money so raised to initiate some significant Christian activity and a meeting place in South Abingdon. To be of real use they felt the project should be organized ecumenically, with the co-operation of the already existing Abingdon and District Council of Churches which comprises the Anglican, Methodist, Congregational, Baptist and Roman Catholic Churches and the Salvation Army in the town and some of the nearby villages.

In putting these ideas into practice and bringing the project even to its present still incomplete stage, it was necessary to have discussions with many bodies besides the Council of Churches, among them the local planning committee of the Borough Council, and a surveyor to look into the possibilities of raising money on the present church. Approval of any action has had to be given by the Abingdon Congregational Church Meeting and the approval and advice of the Moderator of the West Midland Province of the Congregational Church, and the wider bodies of Congregationalism has been sought. Also the church has had to find somewhere else to worship.

The Borough Council, when approached, allotted a plot of land for the scheme. The Council of Churches received the idea with enthusiasm and the Congregational Church asked them to appoint a South Abingdon Committee to assess the need of the area and suggest what form the Christian Venture should take. During the winter 1967–68 this committee consulted clergy, welfare organizations and professional interests in South Abingdon. Local imagination was caught for a spell, reports appeared in the Press and nearby student architects used the planning of a suitable building as an exercise. In the summer of 1968 the appended report was produced. Following this, members of the Council of Churches visited every home in South Abingdon with a questionnaire about the need for some Community Centre and the nature of its activities. Residents were invited to a public meeting which was duly held and an Interim Committee was elected with the Congregational minister as chairman and including the original South Abingdon Committee and a number of people living in South Abingdon.

In the Autumn of 1968 this Interim Committee decided to be less Church centred and to be affiliated to the National Federation of Community Associations. This has now been achieved and the resulting South Abingdon Community Association is completely independent, wishing to erect its own premises. The Congregational minister continues to serve as chairman and the Council of Churches is a Group Member.

Meanwhile the Congregational Church had been discussing some form of association with Trinity Methodist Church which is also centrally placed. This church already operated a coach on Sundays to bring people to its services from South Abingdon. Constitutions of United Churches elsewhere were studied and it was realized that we had a special problem as we wished to retain the two ministers, Methodist and Congregational, both centred on the same Church, Trinity, but with the Congregationalist being greatly involved in an, as yet, unformed, Christian Body in South Abingdon. The fear was expressed that if an outright Union of the Churches occurred, with two ministers at one church, one might be recalled, leaving the South Abingdon venture unstaffed. To overcome this a Partnership Scheme began in July, 1968, with the Congregational Church worshipping with the Methodists. The children's work, youth work, choirs and most weekly meetings were amalgamated but the Congregational Church retained its separate Church Meeting and Finance.

We can thus summarize the present state of the South Abingdon Venture:

1. The Congregational and Trinity Methodist Churches are now in Partnership.

2. An independent Community Association has been formed in South Abingdon as a result of the impetus given by the Council of Churches.

3. Any money available from the disposal of the present Congregational Church building and site could be used to erect a room for use by the Council of Churches for various forms of worship. This would be on the site in South Abingdon allocated by the Borough Council, together with a house for the Congregational minister.

4. Should the South Abingdon Community Association erect its own Community Centre it would be available for hire by the Council of Churches as a group member.

5. The immediate step now is to establish a group of Christians meeting regularly in South Abingdon who will be the nucleus of further ecumenical developments in the area.

## Interim Report of the South Abingdon Committee, May 1968

### I. INTRODUCTION

Early in 1967 the Abingdon Congregational Church decided to lease or to sell its present site in the centre of the town and to use the resulting proceeds to establish a Christian presence in South Abingdon. The Abingdon Council of Churches enthusiastically accepted an invitation to participate in the planning of this venture, for it was the intention of the Congregational Church that the scheme should be truly Ecumenical from the beginning. As a result of the approach to the Council of Churches, a small committee— the South Abingdon Committee—was appointed to advise the Congregational Church and the Council of Churches on the following matters:

    a. the needs of South Abingdon

    b. the nature and range of activities which might be embraced
       by the scheme

    c. organization and leadership

d. the nature of the building

e. the use of the building both on Sundays and weekdays.

## II. CONCLUSIONS AND RECOMMENDATIONS

As this report is intended primarily as a guide to future planning and action it seems right to concentrate on the conclusions and to relegate the procedural matters to a minor role.

The committee reviewed the present and future needs of the whole area of Abingdon south of the River Ock and called on the advice of a number of well qualified people with relevant interests (section III). There are few community facilities in the area at present and it became clear that, in this situation, the aim of the church should be directed towards meeting the whole needs of the community.

In the next few years the increased population of the area will require not only such facilities as we may provide but also other Youth Club and Community Centres as contemplated by both the Borough Council and the County Council. There is, however, an urgent need now for many of the suggested activities and organizations to begin under Christian leadership in whatever premises are available.

*a. General Principles*  Although the majority of the finance for the scheme will be provided by realization of the assets of the Congregational Church, the venture must be truly ecumenical in all its aspects. Nothing must be done to advertise the dis-unity of the Church. The success of the scheme will depend on full and active co-operation of all the denominations represented on the Council of Churches and it is confidently predicted that this adventure in co-operation will be reflected in the whole life of the Church in the town.

*b. General Aims*  In all the activities, both worship and social, the Church must relate its efforts to the real needs of the area and not to try to superimpose any preconceived pattern based on existing practices or prejudices. The scheme provides a unique opportunity to re-discover the position of the Church in society and to relate the Gospel—however obliquely—to the contemporary situation.

*c. Nature of the Scheme*  It follows from the above conclusion that the scheme is most likely to develop into a 'worship centre-cum-community centre'. It is difficult to define it any more precisely at present but it is essential to accept that there must be no insistence on formal church membership as a pre-requisite to participation in any community association activities.

*d. Leadership* If the scheme develops as envisaged in *c* the leader would be an ordained man who will serve both as pastor to the whole community and nominal leader of the community centre. The latter role will not necessarily involve detailed organization of any of the centre's activity but it seems essential to have one person who is recognized as being in overall control. The general oversight of all activities will be exercised by a management committee with the appointed leader as chairman.

At present it seems important that the leader of the scheme would be ordained within the ministry of the Church but this is one of many points which must be recognized as being flexible as the nature of the venture develops, e.g. it might be preferable in time to have a non-ordained leader working closely within a 'Group Ministry' consisting of other ordained clergy within the town.

Initially the appointment of a leader will be the prerogative of the Congregational Church but, in time, it is hoped that this will develop into a Council of Churches appointment.

*e. Buildings* It is essential that any building must have a degree of flexibility in design and use to meet not only the initial demands once they have been established but in order to change with future requirements. Such flexibility might best be achieved through the use of industrial pre-fabricated units which can be arranged in a variety of ways and could be added to quite simply if required. Any buildings which are erected may bear little resemblance to the conventional concept of 'church premises' and it is important to realize that this may be right for the situation.

No land has yet been purchased but the Congregational Church have taken an option on a suitable site of approximately half an acre. Whether or not this option is exercised may depend *inter alia* on the future plans for the use of the Tesdale School Buildings when they are vacated in the early 1970s.

While definite decisions are difficult to make at present, it is important that:

    i work in the area should not await the provision of new buildings and,

    ii every effort should be made to find suitable housing in the area for the leader as soon as possible. Ideally it is recommended that a house should ultimately be provided on the site or close to it.

The committee considered various types of buildings but cannot make any firm recommendations until the nature of the work to be developed has been approved by the Congregational Church in conjunction with the Council of Churches and until the details are more clearly established.

*f. Worship* There should be a clear policy to avoid a pattern of choice between Anglican or Free Church worship at different times on a Sunday. It is recommended that all worship services should be joint Anglican/Free Church with a Eucharistic Service in the morning and a 'Bible Service' in the evening.

The recommendation on a Eucharistic Service would cause some difficulties particularly for the Anglicans, but the minimum situation which could be achieved immediately is as follows:

i Con-celebration, with a clergyman from both the Anglican and Free Churches officiating so that all members of the congregation can communicate, or

ii a service conducted by only one clergyman in which only part of the congregation could communicate but in which otherwise the whole congregation would participate.

Although this is the present position, the Anglican attitude could change rapidly and it is recommended that serious thought should be given to applying for the scheme to be considered as an Area for Ecumenical Experiment.

*g. Finance* The major part of the initial finance will come from realizing the present assets of the Congregational Church but until this is done and the details of the scheme are clearer it is difficult to be certain of either the capital sum required or of the annual running costs. Initially the minimum requirement will be full support of a minister with primary responsibility for the area and it is likely that this could be provided from the income of the Congregational Church.

However, once the legal position is clearer (see *f*) and the venture develops, it will be necessary for each denomination to decide through its own processes what contribution it should make.

*h. Legal Position* The Trust Deeds of the Abingdon Congregational Church are written in such a way to suggest that any of its assets can be used only for the promotion of a Congregational cause. It may, however, be possible to modify this restriction but, if not, the local Congregational Church Meeting has considerable autonomy to determine the future use of any new building, property, land, etc. once it has been vested in a Congregational

Trust Deed. These legal problems could raise difficulties for other denominations wishing to contribute financially to the South Abingdon Venture and a great deal of good-will, faith and mutual trust may be essential if the adventure is not to founder on the strict letter of denominational law!

The Congregational Church is, however, investigating the procedure whereby it could be possible to transfer money from Denominational Trusts to a Council of Churches' Trust. If it proves possible to re-allocate the assets of the local Congregational Church into a Council of Churches' Trust then this could well simplify the position of other denominations.

*i. Management and Organization*  It has been stressed previously that the primary function of the scheme is to meet the real religious and secular needs of the community and it is intended to ascertain these in three ways:

    i through a social survey of the area to be carried out by Culham College.

    ii through a house-by-house visit in the area involving people from all the Churches in the town, and

    iii by a public meeting to be organized in the area following the above visits.

At or following the public meeting it is recommended that an expanded South Abingdon Committee should be formed to develop the details of the scheme. It is suggested that the composition of the Committee and its structure should be as follows:

*General Committee*
Chairman: Minister of the Congregational Church
Representatives from people living in the area—possibly four people, one of whom would serve as Deputy Chairman.
Two representatives from the Abingdon and District Council of Churches—an Anglican and a Roman Catholic.
The members of the present South Abingdon Committee.

*Sub-Committees*
The General Committee will appoint some of its members to form working sub-committees as the need arises, e.g. Building Committee, Management Committee, Activities Committee.

It is recommended that the sub-committees should have the power to co-opt but that the General Committee should be restricted to approximately the numbers given above.

It is also recommended that the following people should be invited to act as Advisory (non-voting) members on the General Committee or on the sub-committees as the need arises.

*Advisory members*
A representative from the Town Council
An architectural adviser
The Area Youth Officer
A representative from each of the following County Departments:
Welfare Service, Children's Department, Probation Service.

The presence of these advisers will ensure that any proposed projects in South Abingdon will be well integrated with any plans of the Borough or County Authorities.

### III. PROCEDURE OF COMMITTEE

The above recommendations and conclusions have resulted from a number of discussions which the South Abingdon Committee held with the following organizations and individuals.

The Town Clerk, Borough Engineer and Chairman of the Planning Committee (Councillor Paxton).

All the clergy in the town—in both formal and numerous informal discussions.

Representatives from the Welfare Services:
Mr Minns, Mr Knight, Miss Goodwin (Probation), Miss Woodger (Welfare), Mr Hobart (Children's Department).

Mr W. Gregson (Culham College).

Architectural Students from the Oxford College of Technology.

The Area Youth Officer, Mr Taylor.

Numerous individuals—too many to mention by name.

### IV. SUGGESTED ACTIVITIES WHICH MIGHT BE DEVELOPED IN THE AREA

As a result of the numerous discussions and conversations the following list gives the range of activities and uses of any buildings which have been suggested. Clearly they provide only a generous framework in which priorities must be established through the enlarged committee suggested above (II, *i*).

Sunday Worship
Play Groups
Youth Clubs/Coffee Clubs

Scouts, Guides, etc.

Townswomen's Guild

Women's Institute

Baby Clinics

Chiropody Centre

Day Centre for Old People

Workshop area for motor-cycle/car maintenance

Provision of general lounge area/coffee bar to encourage social contacts.

Provision of coin-operated washing machines—to help with finances and to provide a social focus.

Baby-minding service during shopping hours.

Baby sitting service in evening.

Establishment of task forces (particularly with young people) to provide help to old and infirm people in area.

Day counterpart of Gio Club, organized by the Welfare Department.

Formation of other groups with like interests, e.g. young mothers.

Focus for sporting activities.

Do-it-yourself instruction for men (women?)

Clearly many more ideas will emerge in the course of time, but an essential requirement for the development of any idea will be the supply of enthusiastic local leadership. The success of the whole venture will depend critically on the local people—the Church will encourage and assist with help from outside the area but the primary requisite for success will be the ability to foster the talent in the local people.

The existence of a vital Christian unity in South Abingdon would be the best possible contribution to providing a new sense of community and cohesion in the area.

# 6. The Roundshaw Experiment

ROUNDSHAW is a rapidly developing new housing estate on the site of the old Croydon Airport. Planned and designed by Clifford Culpin and partners, and built by Wates Ltd., the estate houses around 6,000 people from the London Boroughs of Sutton, Croydon, Kingston and Richmond, and from the housing list of the Greater London Council.

Council housing has been a familiar part of the urban scene since the Housing of the Working Classes Act of 1919, when the opinion was expressed in the House of Commons that the re-housing of poorer people in new estates was an excellent insurance against their indulging in revolutionary activity. Given such negative aims, it is not surprising that many housing estates are little improvement on the slums. As Peter Willmott writes of the Becontree estate, built between the wars to accommodate 95,000 Londoners: 'The visitor to Becontree does not need to be told that he has come to a council housing estate. It has the stamp—the two storey brick terraces, the geometric road patterns, the tame grass, the monotone air. . . . The first view is of endless thoroughfares, lined with straight rows of little houses . . . in the words of one resident "You walk round the streets, and its more or less the same thing all the time" '.[1]

Since 1945, however, the effect of a depressing environment on people's happiness has been taken to heart, and, although the problems of mass housing are by no means over, Roundshaw could be said to have been inspired by the words of the Parker Norris Report on *Homes for Today and Tomorrow*: 'An increasing proportion of people are coming to expect their home to do something more than fulfil the basic requirements. It must be something of which they can be proud, and in which they can express the fullness of their lives. There is an increasingly prevalent atmosphere in which improvements in housing standards will be welcomed,

[1] Peter Willmott, *The Evolution of a Community*, Routledge and Kegan Paul, 1963, p. 1.

and indeed demanded, and in which stress will be laid upon quality rather than mere adequacy.'[1]

Thus, all houses and public buildings in Roundshaw are centrally heated from the one boiler house; all tenants enjoy a generous amount of space; there are plenty of 'extras' like built-in cupboards and wardrobes; some houses have two lavatories, and others have a 'study', though it is doubtful whether it will live up to its name! Outside, the architects have tried very hard to avoid the visual monotony which characterizes so many suburban housing estates; they have mixed industrialized housing with more traditional brick structures, and have varied the height of blocks of flats from three storeys to eleven. And the most striking feature of their design is a pedestrian deck running through most of the estate, which will not only ensure safety, but is also most pleasing aesthetically.

So far as design and technology are concerned, therefore, there is a hopeful future for the Roundshaw Estate; the point should not be underestimated, as discussions with tenants, sponsored by our Experiment, have shown. There is general agreement that a depressing and monotonous environment can have far-reaching effects on people's well-being.[2] It may also blunt their sensitivity to living conditions; as Mr. Graeme Shankland, planning consultant in the re-development of Liverpool, has said: 'Most of our nineteenth and twentieth century environment is so hideous that people have stopped looking at it.' Where, however, the architecture and design are good to live with, it can make a valuable contribution to the formation of a group of people, who are sensitive, critical and optimistic.

Unfortunately, however, there are a number of other factors in the growth of a new housing estate, which may easily militate against so life-enhancing a conclusion. In our Experiment, we have taken it for granted that the Church exists for the promotion of true humanity, and we have believed it to be our responsibility to monitor those incidents and events which have negative effects on people, taking action where this is possible. Our observations so far indicate that the authorities and vested interests who are responsible for the welfare of a growing housing estate may fail in three ways: they may fail to provide plenty of information to incoming tenants about the estate's future; they may fail to provide for consultation with tenants, even though many possibilities for consultation will

---

[1] *Homes for Today and Tomorrow*, HMSO, 1961, p. 3.

[2] See, for instance, the comments of Dennis Johnson in his essay 'Factory Time', in *Work*, ed. Ronald Fraser, Pelican, 1968, p. 14.

still exist in the first eighteen months; and, more generally, there may be a failure in imagination, a lack of sensitivity to conditions of life in a place which is still a building site, lacking many of the amenities which an established area can take for granted.

The work of our Experiment can, therefore, be described under these three headings:

## Information

The leader of the Experiment was appointed, and came to live in the district about a year before the first tenants arrived at Roundshaw. As well as spending a good deal of time learning about the sociology of new areas, he had the opportunity to interview people like the architects, builders and local authorities about the kind of place Roundshaw would be. What amenities would be provided? How would the pedestrian deck work? Where would the people come from, and how much rent would they pay? He found that nobody had any imaginative plans either to 'sell' the estate to prospective tenants, or to tell them about the amenities that would be provided. More serious, although tenants of the GLC would be coming from places as far away as Hammersmith, St John's Wood, and Dagenham, there were no plans to put them in the picture about such vital local services as doctors, shops, clinics, and transport.

This was the origin of a small illustrated booklet 'A Welcome to Roundshaw', sponsored by the Experiment and the local Citizens' Advice Bureau, and given to tenants within forty-eight hours of their arrival. The booklet contains practical information about the nearest post office, the nearest shops for daily and weekly shopping, about where a list of local doctors may be obtained, and so forth. In addition, there is a short account by Clifford Culpin and partners of their objectives in the design of the estate, and a brief history of Croydon Airport compiled by a local librarian. The booklet has proved valuable for new arrivals and is often kept as a 'souvenir' of the move.

When a family first moves into a new estate, it is the immediate practical matters which assume most importance. But once the new carpets have been laid and the new curtains hung, other questions begin to arise. Are there, sometime, going to be shops and schools on the estate itself? Is there going to be a meeting place of some kind? What provision will be made for children and young people? How about a doctor's surgery and a clinic on the estate? This kind of question can, of course, be answered verbally by people who visit the new family, such as the CAB organizer, the health visitor, or the vicar. But, as an estate grows in population, this becomes an increasingly inefficient means of communication; new questions arise, and it is impossible always to be going back to answer them in person.

This situation led to the genesis of the *Roundshaw Courier*, a monthly newspaper, duplicated, for the first eighteen issues, on fourteen quarto sheets, and later appearing as an eight-page tabloid. That the *Courier* has, so far, a 100 per cent circulation on the estate, and that many tenants have kept every issue from no. 1 onwards, is sufficient testimony to the need for such an organ of news and information. The ordained man in a new housing estate has a marvellous opportunity to act as journalist in this way, because, unlike others, he is free to tap the sources of information. In this capacity, he will find himself poring over such documents as council minutes, where news and information lie hidden. Even more, he will write many letters to such people as council officials, architects and builders, in an attempt to prize open their files.

Typical headlines in the *Courier* have been as follows: 'No Schools at Roundshaw till 1969', 'Council sizes up needs of shoppers', 'the shape of things to come', 'Borough Engineer says "no" to crossing at Stafford Road', and so on. It is a common assumption, especially amongst those who work in local government, that people are not interested in decisions made or in the planning of their environment. This very dubious idea proceeds, we believe, from three main causes: first from a basic failure to provide people with information about what is going on; then, when information is provided, it is normally presented in a most unattractive official manner; and, not least, it proceeds from a very low estimate of people's intelligence. The success of the *Courier* proves that new arrivals in a housing estate are interested in much more than signing the tenancy agreement; their appetite for information may be fed, without any kind of patronage, until, as in Roundshaw, there are arguments as to which member of the household shall read the newspaper first.

**Consultation**

John Barr, staff writer for *New Society*, wrote two articles during 1965 under the general title *What kind of homes do people want?*[1] Amongst the most pertinent things he said was the following: 'A

[1] *New Society*, 11 and 18 November, 1965.

community of dwellings does not mean a uniformity of needs, demands, aspirations. The makers of things other than houses have long realised this. They have brought market research to bear; they have troubled themselves to find out what people really want; they have then satisfied those wants. They please the "average" buyer. They must. But they don't ignore all the others. . . . It is, then, ironic that we know much more about people's frivolous wants than about their very serious ones. It is disgraceful that we know more about the kinds of frozen peas, washing powders and cosmetics that people want than about the kinds of homes they want.'

Discussions at Roundshaw, sponsored by our Experiment, would certainly confirm that there are as many different ideas on house-design as there are people! And some architects are now suggesting that the way to meet the needs of individuals is for a 'shell' only to be erected, the tenants themselves deciding on the proportions of the rooms and erecting movable walls, and other fittings. Meanwhile, it is obviously impossible at present for the future tenants or owners to be consulted at the drawing board stage. Planners and people can, however, come together, after the houses have been occupied, for some 'come-back'. We have managed a little of this at Roundshaw, and more is planned. Mr Michael Wates, director of the contracting firm who are building Roundshaw, attended a packed meeting, and listened to the comments and reactions of the earliest tenants; and there is some evidence that the design of some later houses was modified as a result of our conversations. Later, we hope to arrange for similar consultations with the tenants of flats and maisonettes. There are obviously limitations to the effectiveness of this kind of work; but it is a form of bridge-building that modern society needs.

Our consultation with Mr Wates led us to ask whether there were some areas of decision-making in which tenants could and should participate. We discovered that, although some of the amenities would not arrive on the estate for twelve or eighteen months, the authorities had no plans to consult tenants about them. The most glaring instance of this concerned the plans for the bus service. A private argument was conducted between the London Borough of Sutton, and the Wallington Chamber of Trade on the one hand, and the London Transport Board on the other. Should the bus service run between Roundshaw and Croydon only, or should there also be a service to and from Wallington? Each of the vested interests was allowed to put its point of view. The borough wanted a bus to and from Wallington and Sutton so that its services would be accessible; the Chamber of Trade were of the same opinion, because they wished to keep Roundshaw people attending their shops. London Transport were against the proposal on the grounds of economics. At no point in the discussion did it occur to any of these bodies that the inhabitants of Roundshaw had a stake in the matter.

A second example concerns the provision of a community centre. The decision to build this was taken in the very early stages, but the start has been delayed through government cuts in local authority expenditure. Discussions in the estate have shown that many are very suspicious of the idea of a local-authority controlled community centre with a paid warden. There is a strong feeling that such a place would not be 'free'. There is, on the other hand, great enthusiasm for the idea of a working-man's club, like the ones which have operated so successfully in the North East of England. The clash of views presents a good opportunity for proper consultation between planners and people.

The question of participation in planning is not, of course, confined to Roundshaw, but is one of the most pressing problems of the whole of our society. Progress may come, however, if local initiatives are taken in as many places as possible. At Roundshaw, the Experiment has, first of all, attempted to identify those issues where participation is possible; and secondly, it has tried to see that the ideas of Roundshaw people get a public airing, even if no structures exist for officials, councillors and the general public to put their heads together. On the question of buses, the *Courier* ran its own opinion poll in the estate, and transmitted the results to all the appropriate authorities. And, in cooperation with the Roundshaw Tenants Association, the Experiment mounted a public forum on social facilities to which representatives of the borough and of the licencees of the pub were invited so that they could hear, in person, what people were after.

A lively Tenants Association is one of the best possible means of ensuring that people's own ideas penetrate, and the Experiment took the initiative in bringing the Roundshaw Tenants Association to birth. The first arrivals were invited to the leader of the experiment's house to air grievances and put forward ideas, and the Association was immediately formed. At first, all open meetings were held in houses. But as the estate grew it became necessary to hold an open forum in one of the Wates canteens every two months. These are very lively affairs, attended by a very large proportion of the tenants, and they present a marvellous opportunity for the airing of the latest moans and groans, and for the officers of the Association to report on action taken and results gained. An Association which is demanding people's participation in government must ensure that it is itself totally democratic, and in the forum allows for regular consultation between membership and officers. The Experiment shares in the work through the participation of its members, and the columns of the *Courier* are open to all Tenants Association affairs. The two bodies working together have achieved some good results.

## Sensitivity

There exists a whole body of literature describing social change in new housing estates, and the special problems which are associated with new neighbourhoods. The literature[1] reveals a division of opinion amongst the researchers on how far the mental health of people in these estates is any worse than in other areas, and on how far depression and unhappiness may be attributed to the change of environment. But that there are special problems associated with new neighbourhoods, there can be no doubt. Chief amongst them is the feeling of isolation from the outside world which may easily develop, especially amongst people who have moved to their new house from some distance away. Some of this isolation cannot easily be avoided, because it results from the break-up of the 'three-decker' family, and the end of traditional ideas of 'community'; again, over 50 per cent of married women at Roundshaw are out at work every day, either whole-time or part-time; this is unlikely to be reversed, and in certain conditions may increase the loneliness of those who are left behind. Sadly, however, isolation in new housing estates is still compounded by the planners. They are under pressure to build as many houses as costs will allow during a given year, but they have not yet learnt that houses alone do not produce happiness. After eighteen months of life, Roundshaw still has no shopping centre and no bus service. The desire for both these amenities forms part of the basic conversation of every resident.

[1] Amongst the most famous: M. Young and P. Willmott, *Family and Kinship in East London*, Pelican, Revised 1962; J. M. Mogey, *Family and Neighbourhood*, Oxford, 1956; H. Jennings, *Societies in the Making*, Routledge, 1962; J. H. Nicholson, *New Communities in Britain*, National Council of Social Service, 1962; R. N. Morris and J. M. Mogey, *The Sociology of Housing*, Routledge, 1965. See also the *British Journal of Sociology*, passim.

Armed with the slogan 'to make and keep human life human', our Experiment has felt it right to delve as carefully as possible into the 'atmosphere' of Roundshaw, as it changes from month to month. For instance, the *Courier* records the bewilderment of new tenants faced with an unknown locality and surrounded by an environment of mud, noise and chaos; or the loneliness of a housewife, at home for most of the day, with only the opposite house's back fence to look at as she stands at the sink; or the feeling of being in a 'desert', which is produced by living in a place with an 'entrance', marking its difference from the surrounding neighbourhood.

We have, in fact, felt it right to record as many impressions and reactions as possible, however trivial some of them might seem. By so doing we make a point: the development of a housing estate is not just a matter of building technology or of local government finance; a housing estate is a place where human beings, with all their foibles and inconsistencies, are trying to build a new life. It is essential that this should be borne in mind by those who are responsible for 'mass housing'. Conversations are regularly held between the leader of the experiment and members of the contractors' staff; the site managers who took part in these discussions hold that it is their job simply to build as well as possible. There may be different opinions on the propriety of this idea, but it shows that there is a role for somebody to act as 'the conscience' of the architects, the builders and the planners.

There is, of course, a much more positive side of things to be reported. Perhaps the majority of those who move to a new estate are optimistic and lively people who are determined to settle quickly; they will endure the temporary difficulties because of the promise of the future. It is important in these circumstances to have a 'ministry to the strong', and we have attempted this in two main ways. First, the *Courier* is not all 'moans and groans'; it also records the many favourable impressions and tries to catch the sense of excitement which living in a new house generates. More generally, the paper seems to have succeeded in giving Roundshaw a sense of its own identity and dignity, which is important in a borough in which the overwhelming majority of people are owner-occupiers.

In the second place we have tried to provide the conditions where the more positive aspects of social change in a new housing estate may be understood and evaluated. A group of fifteen people meet regularly to discuss 'the meaning of home in modern life', and deal with such subjects as privacy and community, work and home, the effect of environment on people and a good deal else. A syllabus[1] for this study was prepared, and Mr A. R. Center, Staff Officer for Wates-Built homes, acts as group consultant.

A third related activity has also been begun. A Saturday afternoon conference on 'New Housing Estates' was mounted in partnership with the local WEA and attended by local councillors and council officials, architects and social workers. This was our first attempt to come together creatively with local 'principalities and powers', and work in this direction must obviously expand. There is a theological point here, which we have not yet managed to solve. How may the Church at one and the same time take political and other action on behalf of the tenants, and also minister to the needs of those who take far-reaching decisions? At what point should the ministry of reconciliation come into play? Are the interests of those in power and the interests of those at the receiving end of power always irretrievably at variance? These are questions we must work at, if we are to discover the mode of the Church's participation in the modern world.

The Roundshaw Experiment is, of course, often accused of being 'nothing more than social work'. This accusation reveals scant regard for those Christians who happen to be social workers, or indeed for all those Christians who see the focus of their discipleship as lying in the world, rather than within the Church's internal life. As background to our work, however, the Holy Communion is celebrated every week in somebody's house; on this occasion, the insights drawn from our participation in the estate are put alongside biblical insights, and, long term, we should be able to produce a coherent theology of mission and society.

The Experiment is partly ecumenical, being sponsored by Methodists, Baptists, Congregationalists, Presbyterians and the Church of England. It is staffed, at present, only by one ordained Anglican, who has authority from the sponsoring committee to minister to non-Anglicans who belong to the participating denominations. He is paid and housed by the diocese of Southwark. Shortly, a Free Church minister will join him; he will be paid and housed from money raised by the Free Churches centrally and locally. Running expenses for the Experiment are at present provided from the local Anglican church, and go mainly towards meeting losses on the

[1] Obtainable from 1 Brown Close, Roundshaw Estate, Wallington, Surrey, price 5p each.

*Courier.* The paper should shortly become self-supporting, and after that expenses for the Experiment should not be heavy; the possibility of erecting a church building has not been ruled out, but a decision on this will mostly depend on how our experiment in participation develops in the coming years. On present form, it seems very unlikely that we should need one!

# 7. *An Experiment in Church Unity*

## BLACKBIRD LEYS

### The Blackbird Leys Estate

'TEN years ago they used to come out here shooting pheasants'; said the taxi driver as we sped along Oxford's eastern by-pass. 'Now look at it.'

The landscape had changed completely. Gone were the fields, the hedges, the copses. The panorama was now dominated by two high blocks of flats, fourteen storeys high, and, below these, patterned in the manner so characteristic of modern town estates, were innumerable houses.

This area is the Blackbird Leys estate. It lies to the south east of Oxford but within the city boundary. It now provides houses and flats for 10,000 people and it is a potent reminder that Oxford is both a rapidly growing and rapidly changing city. It is estimated that by 1972 a half of all the children in Oxford under twelve years of age will be living on this estate.

Look at a map of the Oxford region made in the 1920s and one sees that neighbouring villages like Headington, Cowley, Marston, and Littlemore were still small, independent communities. Oxford was still a quiet market centre dominated by its university. By 1939 most of these villages had been swallowed up by the spread of the city, largely due to the remarkable development of the motor car industry. This rapid growth has continued today and will, in all probability, continue even more rapidly in the future. The population within the city boundary is now over 107,000. The motor assembly works of British Motor Leyland alone employ over 20,000 people. Oxford, for better or worse, is no longer primarily a university city and if one turns from the groves of Magdalen and the quiet Cherwell one finds a vigorous industrial city and an important regional centre.

As with the growth of so many cities, rapid expansion has

brought many problems—of traffic congestion, slum clearance, and overcrowding. It was with these problems in mind, as well as the influx of workers for the motor factories from other, less fortunate regions, that, in the 1950s the Oxford City Council planned the Blackbird Leys estate, and building began on the land that was formerly Blackbird Leys farm.

The site is spacious and the backcloth of gentle, Oxfordshire hills and beyond them the blue line of the Chilterns is in many ways an attractive setting. But as an entity of people, as a community within the city of Oxford, it suffers from isolation, and is in many ways like an island, for it is separated from the rest of the city by three artificial boundaries—a by-pass, a railway line, and the sprawl of the car factories. There is also only one main access road to the estate.

Today there are two churches on the estate—one which is Roman Catholic and one, the Church of the Holy Family, which was originally built for the Anglican community on the estate but which is now shared between them and the Free Churches. The Free Church pastor and the Anglican priest-missioner work in closest co-operation—as a joint enterprise in all except worship, and united services are held approximately once a month.

The movement towards this sharing, towards the ecumenical ideal has been the result of much thought and generosity from many people and denominations. Contributions towards this experiment in sharing have come from the Lutherans, Quakers, Methodists, Baptists, Congregationalists, and Presbyterians. But the scheme would never have progressed without the generosity of the Anglicans in allowing the church building to be shared with the Free Churches, and without the Congregational church giving a grant to pay for most of the Free Church ministers' stipend. In spite of needs and weaknesses, the church here has begun to live out the gospel of reconciliation within this large, growing, youthful estate. Ones hopes are that eventually it will become fully ecumenical.

As in all new ventures the story of this church is both unusual and, to some extent, complex. It owes its existence to the wisdom of some Oxford churches in seeing their witness in a wider setting, for cities, like people, experience birth, and growth, and death; to the tenacity of certain people in struggling to obviate legal difficulties; to encouragement from people in authority, and to much good will from many quarters.

The ministers, the Revd Mervyn Puleston for the Anglicans, and the Revd Barry Jones for the Free Church community, are widely known on the estate and their pastoral care extends to a great many people not associated with the church. They work extraordinarily hard and their concern for people and their willingness to share in the difficulties and problems of others is an example to us all. It is a sad reflection on society that they are amongst the poorer paid people on the estate. Their labours cannot be measured by 'clocking in' and 'productivity', and few can appreciate the considerable mental strains involved in constantly sharing peoples problems. Within the last year a full-time Anglican social worker has been appointed and a voluntary Free Church worker visits every newcomer on the estate as part of the thirty hours per week she puts in to this work.

The church is already deeply involved in the developing life of the community through its own activities and the participation of both ministers and members in the work of the Community Centre, which adjoins the church.

**Early Developments**

By 1960 the Church of England had decided to take the site offered them by the City Council and build a church. Most of the money came from Anglican funds, though the Pressed Steel Company gave a very generous donation. The story of the Free Church witness and the move towards a sharing of buildings really, begins in 1959 when the Free Church Federal Council produced a brief memorandum concerning the lack of Free Church care within areas of new or recent housing. It was felt that although there were enough churches to serve the needs of a rapidly expanding city, they were not ideally located. It was pointed out that there would obviously be a particular need for Free Church witness on the Blackbird Leys estate, in view of its size. By this time, too, the City Planning Authorities had drawn up detailed plans for the estate and sites had been provisionally fixed not only for Anglican but also for Roman Catholic and Free Churches.

The Free Church Federal Council consequently explored the possibility of a Blackbird Leys church in consultation with the Church of England and the local authority. By late 1960 the two other sites had been taken up and there was an Anglican priest-in-charge, the Revd Peter Malton, living in a council house on the estate, using a temporary hut for worship.

**Closing of Tyndale Congregational Church, Cowley**

One church which faced the problem of effective witness in its own locality was Tyndale Congregational Church, situated on the Cowley Road. Here, in an area of Victorian terrace houses and small shops, it was one of two late nineteenth-century Free Churches who between them served a parish of 9,250 people. Few of its congregation now lived in this part of the city; most of them journeyed by car from other districts and although the church community was alive and forward thinking and by no means few in numbers, it was felt by many of its congregation that the church might well pursue its witness more fruitfully elsewhere and in particular on the newly planned Blackbird Leys estate. Moreover, the church premises needed considerable attention, it being estimated that £5,000 would be needed to put the roof and ancillary buildings of the church in good decorative order.

The minister of Tyndale Church began making tentative inquiries as to possible ways of tackling these problems and also sought the advice of professional bodies. At the Tyndale Church Meeting on 24 February, 1960, he said that the church was faced with three alternatives:

1. To raise at least £5,000 to put roof and buildings in order.
2. To sell the site to a commercial undertaking who would be prepared to build a smaller church or hall in return.
3. To covenant with the Cowley Road Methodist Church (the other Free Church in the locality) to worship and to work together where possible and thus release the value of their own church to start a new church at Blackbird Leys.

Over the next eighteen months a great many plans and possibilities were discussed and investigated by the minister, deacons, and fellowship at Tyndale. They included the re-development of the site with the church, on the first floor, of a new block costing £50,000. The minister was sure that re-development was a practical proposition but after much lengthy deliberation the church members rejected this and also felt that it would not be practicable to link up with Cowley Road Methodist Church.

On 29 November, 1961, at the Tyndale Church Meeting, a vote was taken on the motion, 'We are persuaded not to re-build on the present site but to sell and the money raised to be released for new church building with special recommendation to Blackbird Leys'. Twenty-one members voted in favour and thirteen against.

At a later meeting the Minister, the Revd Lloyd Jenkins, explained that the deacons had held two meetings and had considered all possibilities of the future of the fellowship and they had come to the conclusion that they must recommend to the church meeting that the fellowship should disperse, the members moving to wherever they felt led to attend. The church deacons considered that the end of March would be a suitable date to close.

Two months later, in the final church meeting, the minister explained that under the terms of the trust deeds of the church it seemed that the benefit of the site must pass to the Congregational Church Extension Committee (now the Church Building Committee) and he said that there was little doubt that the committee would be guided by the wishes of the church and the County Union. In this he was to be proved too optimistic for the Tyndale Trust Deeds, dating from October, 1870, were to be something of an obstacle to the wishes of the Tyndale members. These were written in language well nigh incomprehensible to the layman and at the time of closure it had not been fully realized that under them it was necessary to obtain a two-thirds majority at the church meeting before the church could close. Nevertheless the church held its last services on 1 April 1962, and ultimately the church site was leased on a ninety-nine years basis, to be reviewed periodically. The church was demolished and a block of offices with shops on the ground floor were built and the very considerable annual income went to the Chapel Building Society of the then Congregational Union. It was thought that with the money realized from the lease of the site it would be possible to buy the site at Blackbird Leys, to build a manse in the first instant, and to provide the stipend for a minister.

## The Blackbird Leys Council

The courageous act of faith of the Tyndale members in closing their church, and their firm belief in the possibility of development on the Blackbird Leys estate prompted the local Congregationalists to form a committee to explore the possibilities. This committee, the Blackbird Leys Council, initially consisted of representatives of each of the Congregational churches in Oxford, including ex-Tyndale members, and fourteen people attended the first meeting in October, 1962.

Their main task was to fulfil the wishes of the Tyndale members, to examine the type of Christian witness which would best suit an area such as the Blackbird Leys estate, and to establish a Free

Church pastor on it. Although the possibility of using the Tyndale money and developing the site offered to the Free Churches was a positive reality, it was felt by some members that it would be undesirable initially to have two sets of non-Roman Catholic church premises on the estate, bearing in mind that the estate was just developing and that this, from a Christian view, was a frontier situation. This, they felt, could well be an opportunity for creating a partnership of ministers—or, at least, a less conventional witness of the church. It was, however, felt by those who were approached, that at that time in the progress of ecumenism, it would not be possible for the Free Church pastor and the Anglican priest to share the same buildings as this would lead to considerable legal and technical difficulties, and the matter was therefore dropped.

## The Free Church Site

Meanwhile the council was accordingly asked to investigate the possibility of buying the site offered by the Oxford City Estates Surveyor. This was in a prominent position on the estate and 115 ft. by 200 ft. in size. It was originally offered at a concessionary price of £2,400, later to be increased to £3,000. (It should be noted that Oxford is a very expensive city and that land prices are very high.) The Free Church Federal Council had already made tentative enquiries as to the condition of purchase of this site and had applied for it to be reserved for Free Church purposes.

The City Council made it clear that once an option had been taken on the site, building a church must begin in three years. Realizing that there was a considerable degree of urgency in the matter of raising the necessary money and that the Chapel Building Committee might not be in a position to give the money necessary for the building of the church, other, less expensive methods of developing the site were considered. These included buying only half the site and retaining an option on the other half, and building a four bedroomed house which would include a large room for meetings, costing between £6,000 and £7,000 (1963 figures). The Council passed a resolution that they should agree to buy the site, assuming of course that the money was available.

## The Free Church Ministry

Representation was therefore made to the Congregational Union to provide the money necessary for the establishment of a Free Church. The recommendations submitted were that, to begin with, the pastor should live in a council house on the estate until the exact needs of the church be known, enabling him to appreciate the type of building that would be ultimately required, and also the necessary priorities, and that he would be linked with the nearest Congregational church, Temple Cowley, who had agreed to call him an 'associate minister'. Unfortunately at this time the Chapel Building Committee did not have sufficient funds at their disposal to loan the money necessary for the purchase of the site and they also felt that this application was essentially the province of another committee—that of the Maintenance of the Ministry, since it was normally necessary to establish a pastor and a worshipping community before building a church. There were obvious difficulties here because normally the Maintenance of the Ministry Committee only supported applications from established worshipping Free Church communities—and here there was none. There were also some doubts about the legal validity of the Tyndale money being used at all for a cause such as that envisaged on the Blackbird Leys estate.

Fearing that it might be difficult to raise the necessary money the committee considered the feasibility of a part-time ministry, but this, after much discussion, was not felt to be a satisfactory solution since, if the ministry was worth establishing at all on Blackbird Leys it should be worth doing on a full time basis. It was also strongly felt that if the venture was to be truly representative of the Free Churches other denominations should be approached and asked to participate. The Presbyterians had already shown considerable interest in the scheme and the minister of St Columba's Presbyterian Church, Oxford, joined the committee in January, 1964, along with Presbyterian lay representatives.

## Legal Difficulties—Tyndale Trust Deeds

At this stage, however, there were difficulties over the next steps to be taken. No positive reassurance had been received from the Congregational Union that the money from the sale of the Tyndale premises could be used to further a church on the Blackbird Leys estate. Therefore no positive progress could be made towards buying the site. The committee therefore re-examined the legal situation concerning the Tyndale Trust deeds and also made plans for further representation to London. If, in some respects, this was a time of disillusionment amongst some of the committee members they were much encouraged by many gestures of approbation for the scheme; notably that the Presbyterians had shown much sympathy and earnestly wished to support the scheme, and the Oxford Congregational churches continued in their strong conviction as to the rightness of the cause. £220 had now been raised and there had also been a most generous interest-free loan of £1,500.

The Tyndale trust deeds proved to be complex and old fashioned and it was only at this late stage discovered that technically Tyndale should not have closed, since the Trust Deeds stated that there must be a two-thirds majority in the vote. It was also discovered that there were Model Trusts which could be applied for and which give more up to date administrative powers to the trustees whilst not altering the general picture. Yet it was still not clear whether the money could be used to finance a pastor rather than simply building a church and whether the money could be used to support a Free Church pastor of a denomination other than Congregational.

## Sharing the Church

In retrospect one suspects that concentration upon the niceties of the Tyndale Trust deeds proved to be a mistake. These ultimately did not enter into the financial arrangements governing the appointment of a Free Church pastor but the committee was particularly conscious of the part played by the ex-Tyndale church members in this venture. The Congregational churches within Oxford also strongly pledged their support to the venture and passed resolutions to that effect.

Other types of witness had also been discussed at church meetings, particularly the development of 'buildingless churches', so much so that in October, 1964, a resolution was passed by the committee 'That being convinced that we do not envisage the necessity of a church building, and that, assuming a manse to be eventually available, we relinquish the church site originally offered by the City Council'.

At this meeting also, the Anglican priest of the estate, the Revd Peter Malton, became a full member of the committee.

This ecumenical mood was given further impetus by a resolution, passed without opposition and with considerable enthusiasm, at a meeting of the Oxford Council of Churches, asking that 'The Oxford diocese and corresponding bodies of other churches designate the Blackbird Leys estate as an area of ecumenical group ministeries in the sharing of buildings and equipment and the development of mission'. It was moved by the then vicar of Cowley and seconded by the Revd Peter Malton.

There can be little doubt that the mood and decisions made at the conference on Faith and Order held at Nottingham that year greatly influenced this step. There were doubts as to whether the Anglicans could allow, by law, Nonconformists to worship in their buildings, and it was later explained that it would be necessary for the Anglican church to be dedicated and not consecrated.

Strengthened by these assurances the committee felt that they were, after an appeal to the Free Churches in the Oxford area, in a position to finance a man for a year or at least for eighteen months, and matters moved with considerable rapidity from then onwards.

### Free Church Links with the Anglicans

It was now felt by many that it would be most unfortunate if the Free Churches, in erecting their own building, were to find themselves unconscious rivals to the Anglicans. Moreover, the cost of building could be enormous. Consequently, the Blackbird Leys Council agreed, after much deliberation, that there was no real necessity of a church building in the traditional sense, and, assuming a manse to be eventually available, the Free Churches decided to relinquish the church site originally offered.

By this time, the Anglicans had almost completed their church building situated next to the Community Centre at a cost of approximately £38,000, an impressive example of modern architecture with a curved roof possibly inspired by Le Corbusier's remarkable church at Ronchamp in France (Notre Dame du Haut). The priest-in-charge had shown much sympathy towards a sharing of buildings. Nevertheless, if there were any possibility of sharing buildings, legal difficulties would have to be overcome and it would be necessary to dedicate rather than consecrate the church. At this time the Anglican priest was greatly helped by a worker priest.

Accordingly it was agreed to meet the Bishop of Oxford to discuss the possibility of closer links, and, as a first step the Bishop, in consultation with the parishioners on the estate, had generously agreed to dedicate rather than consecrate the church.

The Bishop gave the venture powerful support. There was, he felt, an almost unlimited need for evangelization in the widest sense, but in order to avoid any misunderstandings, certain stipulations were laid down, particularly concerning church services.

In the meantime, arrangements continued with the Congregational Union in London for the financing of a Free Church pastor, though this was not without technical difficulty. The payment of clergy from central funds depended upon there being present a gathered community of church members with a church building. Blackbird Leys had none of this, and much rethinking had to be done in committee. Nevertheless by the Spring of 1965 arrangements had been made for the financing of the pastor with the major contribution coming from the Congregational churches central fund. There were also important contributions from local sources—from Anglicans, Presbyterians, Methodists, Baptists, Congregationalists, Quakers, and Lutherans, and there were now representatives of all these denominations except the Lutherans on the Blackbird Leys Council, as well as members from the estate. The Presbyterians also raised money to pay off the remainder of the debt on the Anglican church.

On 29 September, 1965, a young Congregational minister, the Revd Barry Jones, was inducted to be the Free Church minister on the estate, at a service attended by the Bishop of Oxford and representatives of many denominations in the locality.

## The Church Today

Apart from separate Anglican and Free Church services, the ministers work in closest co-operation in sharing the work on the estate.

The Free Church minister lives in a council house. From a financial viewpoint this is not entirely satisfactory since it would be better to purchase a house and this is not financially possible, but it does mean that he lives in a dwelling on the estate with exactly the same physical conditions as most of his neighbours. thus, in some ways, making it easier to identify with them.

Thus was formed a church shared between Anglicans and Free Churches in which they are able fully to share in their hopes and responsibilities and to develop an important experiment in team ministry and the sharing of buildings.

It would be difficult to summarize the work of the church on an estate of 10,000 without relating it to the lives of the people as a whole.

Although ecumenical progress is such that it has not yet been possible for combined services to take place, there is nevertheless much opportunity for the development of less orthodox patterns of worship, and in an area where few attend regularly, there is perhaps more questioning as to the true meaning of worship and its relevance to life in the 1970s. Thus, there is considerable care over the simplicity of language, and a greater attempt to get some degree of involvement by the congregation.

Few people, in comparison with the size of the estate, worship. People already with close church connections tend to worship in the 'old' church, and it is true to say that working class areas are not noted for their support of the non-Roman churches. Yet it is surely significant that young people form a much greater percentage of the congregation than in most churches and more adults have been attracted than in many well-established churches over a similar period.

The church, too, has been able to play an important part in the working of the Community Association and therefore a prominent part in the social awareness of the estate. The chairman of the executive is a church warden, the secretary the Anglican priest, the president, the Free Church minister, and the vicar's wife works as assistant warden. A Boys' Brigade, and a Youth Group (for those not attached to any in the Community Centre), have been established, and the parish meeting combines the function of the Parish Council and the Church Meeting. There are also a number of other organizations which include a Coffee Club for mothers with small children.

Yet there are many broader problems connected with the estate which offer the church considerable challenge. It still suffers from geographical isolation, being divided from the rest of Oxford by a motorway. Apart from the old peoples home (where services are regularly held and with which there is much contact) practically all the adults are of a similar age group—mostly parents of young children, and it is not fully realized that by 1972 one in three children in the city of Oxford under twelve will be living on the estate.

There are, too, problems connected with employment which, with the constant demand for greater productivity in the motor industry, are not fully realized. Many wives go out to work to supplement their husband's income, but the provision for play groups appears to be wholly inadequate. Many of the men work at night, yet the social consequences of night shift working have yet to be seriously evaluated. They can undoubtedly cause considerable friction in a household of many children where father wishes to sleep during the daytime.

The fear of redundancy can also greatly influence peoples' attitudes. The motor industry is not noted for giving ample warning before laying off employees, and the traditional weekly pay packet does not bring the security of the monthly salary.

Within the context of the estate the church clearly has a very important role to play and those within its organization are conscious of the great advantages to be gained from working together and sharing buildings. It is, too, conscious of the great amount of pastoral work to be done, and for this reason a full time social worker was appointed in October, 1968, and there is also a part-time worker.

## Problems of the Ecumenical Church

The growth of the ecumenical enterprise, too, has many problems, for its goals are too frequently obscured by legal difficulties, and from lack of funds. The church is unlikely to be self-supporting for many years to come. It is difficult for many people, who have not been brought up in the spirit of giving, to realize that in order to finance the church and the pastorates costs £3,000 per annum. The estate can only raise about one-third of this at present, and whilst a part cause of this may be the youthfulness of the locality, it has to be remembered that the continuance of the Church of the Holy Family depends upon the generosity of many organizations outside the estate, particularly at present, the Church of England and the Congregational Church.

Much thought has been given to the ecumenical idea and of its vision and brotherhood. It is the hope of those concerned with the Blackbird Leys venture that eventually a truly ecumenical church will be established, but the present progress is sadly hindered by legal and other difficulties and we seem to stumble our way over many of the detailed practical problems of the ecumenical church which have not yet been worked out.

For instance, how does one become a member of an ecumenical church in 1970? At what age should a young person become a member? Does one affiliate to all other denominations so that one can be a member of each one? Before this can be done, it is presumably necessary for a constitution to be drawn up by the local church agreeing on the principles of Baptism, Confirmation, Membership, Lay Participation, etc.

And how does one go about appointing a minister to a church which technically does not have any members, since the ecumenical church is non-denominational? Since one of the main intentions of the Blackbird Leys enterprise is towards greater unity it was felt by many on the council that the Free Church ministry should be shared between all the denominations and that a Congregationalist, for instance, should be followed by a Presbyterian, so that each denomination would have some share. Ideally there should be some ecumenical fund for all such experimental work but this is not possible since the monies in the hands of the denominations can, mostly, only be used for the work of that specific denomination. Thus Congregational money must, by and large, be used to finance a Congregational minister. Moreover, there usually has to be a gathered community before funds are given. If the church is truly ecumenical its members will not be of any specific denomination, so further legal problems may occur. These are, of course, being tackled, but all too often the thinking is ten years ahead of the legalities, even though great progress has been made. This will continue, and already a group is at present meeting in London to see how the ministry in new areas and ecumenical pastorates can be supported by the main Free Churches.

## Conclusion

On the estate there is still much apathy towards some important issues and getting local people involved has not always been so successful as one might hope. Leaders from within the estate are few. The Blackbird Leys Council, with its representatives from local Quakers, Baptists, Presbyterians, Congregationalists, Methodists, and Anglicans meets about four times a year to advise the Free Church side. One-third of its representatives come from the estate. It is still responsible for appointing a Free Church minister, but with the strengthening of the local church its function is no longer so important as formerly.

Thus has the Church of the Holy Family witness grown and developed. It did not begin as an ecumenical enterprise; it is still not truly ecumenical, though it is to be hoped that this will be its ultimate aim. Its story shows clearly how important resolutions and events, like the Nottingham Faith and Order Conference, can help and influence the local situation. It brings to light many of the problems which face the Church today—lack of money, lack of leaders, public apathy. It also highlights some of the strengths which sharing can give—a sharing of problems, of resources, of ideas, and a greater mutual understanding between denominations.

It is encouraging that this enterprise, which involves a sharing of practically all church activities between Anglicans and Free Churchmen, should have been helped locally by so many denominations both at a local and a national level. Its history shows particularly how much attitudes towards unity and interdenominational understanding have changed in the last few years.

# 8. *Youth and Community*

## AN EXPERIMENT AT ST PETER'S METHODIST CHURCH, GILLINGHAM

### The Setting

GILLINGHAM is a town of some 80,000 inhabitants, which forms part of the Medway Towns conurbation, with a total population of about 250,000. The area is in Kent, thirty-five miles from London, on the south bank of the Thames estuary. The geographical relation between the Medway Towns is similar to that between the London Boroughs, in that it is difficult, for example, for a stranger to know when he is in Gillingham, rather than Chatham, or in Chatham rather than Rochester. In terms of local government, however, each town is a separate borough, and there is no overall local authority for the conurbation.

Traditionally, the towns have been dominated by Chatham Dockyard (which is situated in Gillingham) and by the Armed Services (Army, as well as the Navy). Until recently, the dockyard was the only large employer of labour, and it is still by far the largest, as much of the nation's dockyard work has been concentrated there. In the past fifteen years, however, there has been an influx of medium size engineering and electronic industries, which are increasingly significant for the labour patterns of the area. A recent government report singled out the Medway Towns as containing the most concentrated development of engineering and electronic industries in the south east.

Gillingham is the major residential area for this labour force, and also has a growing community of London commuters, who mainly live in the newer fringe areas and estates. The older central area of Gillingham, where St Peter's is situated, consists largely of rows of terraced or semi-detached property, dating from the Edwardian era or early twenties—bay windows, small front gardens, often with basements, attics and cellars. The major shopping and commercial area is in Chatham, which is the central town of the Medway area.

Community leadership has never been strong in this area. Many families have belonged to the area for generations, and the bread winners have always worked in the dockyard, and sons have tended to follow their fathers in the same direction. Those who desire promotion and have ambition, have often to be prepared to move about to other naval dockyards; this has meant that there are many links with other dockyard towns, e.g. Portsmouth and Rosyth. Naval and military families, again, are generally 'birds of passage', and therefore tend to form their own communities rather than playing a part in the neighbourhood generally. The present problems of community in the area tend to centre around the clash and tension between the older, rather insular, dockyard-orientated community, and the newer, expanding, socially mobile and flexible community which has come into the area as a result of the more recent industrial development, and the attraction of the area as convenient and relatively cheap for house-purchasing and commuting.

Methodism in the area has never been strong, and, in particular, lay leadership has always been something of a problem. This, perhaps, is related to the nature of the traditional pattern of community as described above. Until 1966, there were two circuits in the area, the Chatham Mission Circuit covering Chatham and Rochester, and the Medway Towns Circuit covering Gillingham, Strood, and some country village churches. In 1966 the Chatham Central Hall was closed, and the two circuits amalgamated. The new Medway Towns Circuit covers the whole area, has a membership of 1,150, and five ministers, with a total of ten churches within the Towns, and six small village churches. The main strength of the circuit lies in the Gillingham part of the area. The minister responsible for St Peter's has responsibility for one other church.

### How the church came to begin renewal

In 1961, we had two churches in central Gillingham, both weak and declining in membership and effectiveness. The one redeeming feature was the lively youth work being done in both churches. My predecessor, the Revd Donald White, was the first minister to have charge of both churches, and he gave leadership in the direction of amalgamation. This was achieved in 1963, with a plan for selling one church and premises, and modernizing the other with enhanced facilities for youth work. At this time, Mr Terry Walton was Field Officer for MAYC in the South East District, and he pressed for the development of the new premises as a full scale Youth Centre, with a full-time leader, and an emphasis on contacting the 'unattached' young people of the area. Mr Walton met several times with Leaders and Trustees, and with the Circuit Quarterly Meeting. At about the same time, a series of evening services in the newly united congregation were devoted to considering the Church's mission. As a result of all this, the original plans were expanded to include this concept of a Youth Centre, and Government and LEA support was obtained. The newly reconstructed building was opened in June 1965, and I came as minister in September of that year.

## How it works

From the beginning it was planned that the Project should involve the whole congregation, rather than just a few concerned people. The management of the Centre is based on an occasional consultation of all who are concerned in the work of the Centre, where a free discussion of problems and developments takes place, without a set agenda. In the early days of the Project these were held quarterly, but latterly twice a year has been usual. Attendances at these vary from thirty to eighty, all of whom are in some way involved in the work. Over the four years of the Centre's existence, attendances at this have gradually reduced, as the first flush of enthusiasm has died, and as the work of the Centre has both developed and changed. The membership of St Peter's Church during this period has always hovered about the 150 mark. The workers include some people from other churches in the Circuit, as this was conceived as a Circuit Project in the beginning. There is a Centre Management Committee, which also includes representatives from other churches, as well as the LEA. Each area of work that has been developed has its own sub-management committee responsible to the Centre committee, and these also include appropriate representatives of the wider community. These areas of work include Old People's Luncheon Club, Toddlers Play Group, and the Youth Centre itself.

At the beginning, youth work was the only activity envisaged, but a desire to develop in other directions was soon expressed by some people involved. This desire was taken up by inviting a Health Department official to meet with interested people to discuss the needs in the community in the area of Old People's Welfare, the Senior Health Visitor to discuss what was needed in the area of under-fives' welfare, local Church youth leaders to discuss the possibility of ecumenical youth group development, and so on. It was as a result of these consultations that the work in these areas was developed alongside the development of youth work. This process was begun in the winter of 1965–66.

The Youth Centre has had a chequered history over the past four years, operating for periods with much apparent success in terms of numbers and activities, and then, at other periods, relapsing into an almost moribund state. A number of factors have contributed towards these fluctuations. For various reasons, there was a rapid succession of full time leaders in the first two years, and therefore a failure to provide strong, continuing leadership. As the project got under way, it became apparent that there was a conflict of aims and expectations amongst many who were helping in the Centre. This meant withdrawal from the project by some people, and waning enthusiasm on the part of others. This lack of leadership and lack of a sense of direction has affected the whole operation at various times in the past four years. An Ecumenical Youth Group ran very successfully as part of the Centre for about eighteen months. This was fifty to sixty strong, and represented most church traditions. This particular project, which, unlike the rest of the Youth Centre, was specifically for church-oriented young people, finally foundered on the conflicts that arose between young people from churches with a strong Conservative-Evangelical flavour, others who were cast in a more Radical mould, and some whose church tradition had not given them any particular attitude to scripture or mission.

The development in old peoples welfare work and in the toddlers play group has been much more consistent, and has not had any similar problems. The Luncheon Club was the pioneer in this field in the area, and it has led to several others being established, and to a scheme for the building of a Day Centre being launched. Those who have been involved in the Luncheon Club work have as individuals and as a group given a considerable impetus to the whole development in this field in the Medway Towns. The Club has been full to capacity from the beginning. A similar situation obtains with the Toddlers Play Group. The only obstacle to a great deal more development in these fields has been the limitations of the building, which was not designed for these kinds of activities.

**The present situation**

The Youth Centre operates for five evenings a week, and for the past twelve months has been led by two part time leaders. This has been a deliberate policy, to operate for a temporary period. We have been able to sponsor an experienced voluntary leader, whilst he underwent a training course in full time Youth leadership. At this present time (Summer, 1969) the Youth Centre has a membership of some 250, and is probably operating somewhere near its capacity as far as numbers are concerned. Its function is now more clearly seen as a leisure centre rather than an 'activities' centre, and we are now entering into a new phase of co-operation with the LEA Youth Service. The St Peter's full time leader will work as a member of a team within the Borough under the leadership of the Senior Youth Leader. The aim is to use the facilities that are available at St Peter's and at the LEA Youth Centre in the area in a complementary way rather than as separate and sometime rival institutions. It is also envisaged that the team concept will enable the professional skill of youth leaders to be used to the best advantage according to the needs and opportunities of youth in the area.

At St Peter's Youth Centre, there is a team of voluntary assistants, helping in various ways with the running of the Centre. These are drawn from all sections of the congregation, including even the traditional Women's Meeting. The involvement of a considerable section of the membership in the running of the Centre rather than of just a group of enthusiasts is probably the chief distinction between this and otherwise similar Centres that exist in Methodism.

**Renewal in the life of the church**

Whilst the development of what is now a Youth and Community Centre is the outstanding aspect of what has happened at St Peter's, this development has led to considerable changes in the traditional pattern of church life. The worshipping community has not developed numerically. It is fairly static, seventy to eighty in the evening congregation and thirty to forty in the morning. Communion is twice a month with almost the whole congregation remaining to communicate; this is assisted by a revised order of worship, that emphasizes the character of the Sunday service as a Pre-Communion, even on those occasions where the Sacrament is not celebrated. A good deal of experimentation in worship has been done, with the use of modern music and drama. The participation of the congregation in all this has been encouraged, and, after a good deal of initial hesitation and caution, the congregation now generally expects to be involved as participants rather than spectators. A house group scheme has operated for three years; this has involved a minority of the congregation, but has opened up the whole field of thinking about Christian belief and practice in a new way. A regular programme of Bible study is being developed, and this is related to the discoveries about the needs and the nature of the local community which have been made. The church often reveals an un-selfconscious awareness of the community, which is, in my experience, rare in church communities.

A detailed community survey was conducted in the ward where the church is situated at Easter, 1967. The help of the Order of Christian Witness and of students was obtained from this, and we had the advice of a professional sociologist. The results were of great interest to many people in the community, not least the Borough Health and Welfare departments. The intention was that future development of the church's life should be based upon the information and insights gained, but, in fact, this has not happened. I think this is partly due to the church not being anchored to as closely defined an area as a ward, and partly due to the fact that the church community was coping already with about as much as it was able.

Between 1965 and 1968 the church was coping with a heavy debt on the rebuilding scheme that had already been completed. This was because the sale of redundant buildings did not realize the sum that was originally expected. The debt was finally wiped out by the beginning of 1968, so a Stewardship scheme was then launched with the help of the Methodist Stewardship Organization, and this has resulted in a healthy, well-managed financial set-up, and in an enlargement of the team of people involved in the whole project.

### Snags and criticisms

1. Lack of leadership is a problem. St Peter's does not have any teachers or professional people in its congregation, and only a few who manage their own small businesses. We are short of people who are accustomed to taking initiative and responsibility. Too much, therefore, still depends on the minister and one or two other people as managers and administrators.

2. Another problem is the aspect of the venture which was conceived as a 'Circuit Project'. The scheme could never have started except as a Circuit Project, because St Peter's was thought to be too

small and weak a church to sustain it on its own. As time has passed, however, the whole venture has been seen increasingly as a 'St Peter's scheme by the rest of the circuit. In a way, this was inevitable, as the community at St Peter's is the one that is constantly involved in the whole process of renewal that has been entailed, and the other churches have not been involved in the whole process of experience and experiment that has taken place. Other factors have been (a) the amalgamation of circuits that took place in 1966, which meant that several churches in the circuit now were not involved in the original planning that goes back to 1963; (b) the changes in ministerial personnel, who were also not involved in these original discussions; (c) the other legitimate needs for mission and outreach that claim the attention of the circuit, e.g. the challenge of the changing nature of the community, and the considerable new areas of housing development; and (d) the constant tendency of churches to revert to an insular, introverted attitude towards their life and worship.

3. Despite the large percentage of people at St Peter's who are involved in the work of the Youth and Community Centre, there is still a non-vocal (in public, at least) opposition to the whole scheme, and to everything that has happened in recent years. It is a small minority, but, nevertheless, still there—and looking for faults and mistakes (of which, of course, there have been plenty!).

4. The majority of people probably still see the Church's mission in terms of individual conversion and/or an increase in congregations attending for traditional Church worship patterns. The presence of a large and 'successful' Anglican Conservative Evangelical church nearby, which has a good measure of success with young people (within the terms of its understanding of its purpose) underlines this problem. There is always the temptation to cast envious glances at the secure and well-trodden paths of work that can be followed in this sort of church life.

5. There is, anyway, the tendency to look for results in some measurable and quantitative way. Particularly when problems arise that are difficult to cope with, there is the temptation to want to stop attracting the less socially acceptable young people, because they are too 'difficult', and to try to cater for so-called 'respectable' (i.e. amenable) young people from whom we might expect more success in Conservative Evangelical terms.

6. There is the danger that we may be kidding ourselves that we have gone out to the world to get involved and to serve, when, in reality, we have only brought a bit of the world on to our church premises in order to tame it.

7. The difficulty and costliness of youth work with the 'unattached', not sufficiently realized at the scheme's inception.

8. About forty people are involved in our House Group scheme, in consultations, in Bible Study, and in policy discussions at Leaders' Meeting and Management Committee level. The Faith is discussed, our conception of mission is worked out, and our theological approach to the Church's work is explored. The problem is that a gap tends to appear between those involved in this process, and those whose involvement in the actual work of the Centre often means that they are not present at such discussions. So, all too easily, a division grows between those thinking about theory, and those involved in practice. We can easily find ourselves not practising what we preach, or not preaching what we practise!

9. Relations with other churches, Methodist and otherwise. There is bound to be controversy over the ethos of our work and its objectives, especially in an area where the three chief strands of churchmanship appear to be Edwardian Anglo-Catholicism, extreme Conservative Evangelicalism, and comfortable midstream nonconformity. Minister, church and congregation are very vulnerable to pangs of self-doubt, and not always well-equipped to meet criticism.

What has been attempted at St Peter's is a renewal of the Church in terms of

    *a.* Structure and Organization (the application of social group methods and non-directive leadership)

    *b.* Work (the orientation of the church towards a purpose lying outside itself)

    *c.* Worship (the development of properly indigenous and relevant forms).

This Renewal has started in every area of the church community's life. In some areas, not a great deal has been achieved; in others, quite a lot. There have been setbacks and disappointments, and there has been success, and unexpected new insights have been gained. It has been, and is, an experiment. In the end, it may all collapse, or it may move on to something more. But, whatever happens, I am sure that this is how the Church needs to live, and also how it needs to die, if it is to be the instrument of Christ.

# 9. The Lune Street Experiment, Preston

T E N years ago the 'Lunes Street Experiment' was begun in a 'downtown' church in Preston, Lancashire. The church selected had a long and significant history in the North West. Opened in 1817, rebuilt in 1861, it had a begrimed frontage, which, after cleaning, revealed an imposing facade supported by large corinthian columns. The site was close to the centre of the town and the plan was to create a 'Central Church' to serve this large urban industrial community.

Through the vision of Leonard Tudor, then General Secretary of the Methodist Home Mission Department, and the support of money from the Joseph Rank Benevolent Trust, large scale alterations and modifications were made to the interior and front entrance and approach. New cinema-type seating was put into the old chapel. A large foyer was constructed, the usual offices were built and ancillary accommodation improved. It was planned as a meeting point for Methodists and others from the outlying districts, as well as a place of worship and service for the town.

The urban renewal programme of the Local Authority has entailed the virtual demolition of the inner shopping area of Preston. Old buildings have been and are still being replaced by modern shops and offices. A new shopping precinct has been developed opposite the front entrance to the chapel. The street in which it stands has largely been rebuilt. The front of the church has been used by the town planners as the focal point of the main thoroughfare of the new shopping precinct. People walking along this main pedestrian way are led by eye and step through the imposing entrance to the doors of the Central Church. These civic alterations to the central area of Preston have literally put Lune Street Chapel physically 'on the map'.

As the District Chairman has written, 'a "down-town" chapel has been transformed into a lively and popular Central Church'.

The physical setting and geographical position is a vital matter, but the church is not merely bricks and mortar or position, *it is people*. To this end a minister and deaconess were appointed and they began to create, according to their own terms of reference, a vigorous, lively, popular preaching place. After nine years hard and un-remitting toil Central is a focus for Methodist worship and witness in the whole area.

Under the leadership of the Revd Thomas Jenkinson the worshipping community has grown from small beginnings to a sizeable congregation. His popular folksy-style preaching and the hearty singing, together with many 'specials' gathered a crowd in evening worship, at a time when evening congregations were rapidly shrinking in so many places. In the early days of the experiment, the nucleus was created out of the residue of congregations drawn from several Methodist causes which were closed in the inner area of Preston. These groups were integrated into the small Lune Street congregation. If it has ever been true that 'a crowd attracts a crowd' it certainly has been shown at Central during the nine years of Mr Jenkinson's ministry.

A coffee bar was opened and every day of the week visited by people from far and near. For some this is their first introduction to the fellowship of Central. Youth Club, devotional groups, an SOS Anonymous Telephone Service attempts to listen to, and counsel, people who come in need. Many organizations, Moral Welfare, Blood Donors, etc., avail themselves of the facilities offered by the premises as well as Methodist Church District Administrative Committees.

A Christian Stewardship Campaign during the last two years of Mr Jenkinson's ministry gave good results. Amongst the congregation is a sprinkling of West Indian folk, and, from time to time, people of other nationalities and denominations. A church that had almost expired has come to life, and through countless efforts by the minister, deaconess and people, a significant positive Christian witness has been made at the heart of the County Borough of Preston and district. This urban conurbation comprises, as well as Preston, the Urban districts of Fulwood, Penwortham, Longridge and Walton-le-dale, a total population of over 200,000 people.

**Ingredients of 'success'**

What have been the ingredients of success of the scheme to re-habilitate a down-town church and develop it into a centre which serves the town? The present position has been reached by the cumulative effect of numerous factors.

1. The time was ripe for innovation ten years ago. Either Lune Street closed its doors, or used the opportunity to initiate an experiment which would involve the renewal of the physical structure of the building, and a new programme for Christian work, initiated in the new setting.

2. The chance to rationalize Methodist work in the centre of Preston at that time was grasped. Five expiring Methodist causes were closed. People from these chapels joined in with the small number of folk at Lune Street, to form the nucleus of a new congregation.

3. Considerable Connexional and District support was sought for the scheme (around £20,000) and obtained for an experiment.

4. An energetic popular style personality was called to lead the experiment. The Revd Tom Jenkinson, at the height of his powers, whilst traditional in approach, is a lively and hard working man of the people with 'the common touch'.

5. The minister was given *carte blanche* to attempt the project. He was offered and exploited to the full his freedom of action, and with a deaconess concentrated at this one point.

6. There was a handful of capable and devoted key workers who supported the scheme and backed up their leader in his work. This factor must *not* be minimized. It has been very important to the success of such a venture. Conservative attitudes were overcome but not without pain.

7. The scheme was built originally on the vision of people not directly involved in the actual day to day work. They had prepared the way, and gave it moral and financial backing. Previous ministers, the District Chairman, the General Secretary of the Home Mission Department, the Chapel Committee, the District Officers and laymen all gave valiant moral support. This group of people were sensitive to the situation, with a capacity to see and hear and feel the challenge of the moment.

8. The leader clearly saw opportunity to which many were blind. He and two or three others had the capacity to stretch their perceptive powers, the knack to fully exploit the opportunity as they saw it. They developed the mental flexibility to adjust quickly to the changing situation as the experiment proceeded. Within a traditional frame, they were prepared to innovate.

9. In the last phase of the experiment under the original leader, they accepted and began to exploit the Christian Stewardship programme. Through this project a whole new scheme of work was

started at a moment when the original ideas needed to be examined afresh in the light of the evidence emerging from the ever new and changing scene in which the church was attempting to do its work.

10. Popular preaching with humour and parable played an important part in the scheme. Ten years ago there was, and to some lesser degree still is today, a considerable amount of religion in this part of the North West. The popular preacher can still make some impact upon an older generation which is religiously conservative and traditional in approach to church life.

## Working concepts

This then was the picture when I came to be minister at Central a year ago. The people of the church had come a long way since the 'fresh beginnings' nine years previously. Where do we go from here? Do we look for some new gimmick which will 'hold' the congregation? Is preaching alone enough? It is hard to spell out to people who feel they have a prescription for 'success' that the Church in Britain is in retreat. 'We're not', they retort. 'It's different here!'

In thinking and planning for the future do we need to stay as we are, or is change essential to meet the new challenges that are constantly thrusting themselves at us in a changing and unstable world? It was soon obvious to me that if the prescription for success is so closely identified with one personality as the work had been in this case, then when that 'figure' departs, people go through a period of 'the jitters'. They try to mask their fear . . . fear that with the departure of 'the man', perhaps the faithful who have filled the pews while he was there in the flesh to instruct, lead and entertain them, will also depart. Such neurotic tendencies are not rare in Methodism. Perhaps this is the weakness of much of our understanding of Ministry and Mission. Perhaps we have been too dependent on the strong charismatic authoritarian personality, expecting him to work the oracle, 'deliver the goods', and 'fill' the church.

One thing I was sure about as we faced the future—we should face it together. I felt certain that within this sizeable, largely minister dependent community, there would be untapped reservoirs of social energy, specialized skills and resource. This potential needed to be discovered, mobilized and used to strengthen the 'effective' mission of the church. Somehow the total community needed to be made aware of its responsibility for the Mission, and involved in the planning and the carrying through of the Mission. They had made a start in congregational participation through the recent Stewardship Campaign. They needed to be encouraged further to explore together how they could minister to the needs of the society around them. Rather than seeing themselves as a community ministered unto, they needed to be made aware that the Church exists 'not to be ministered unto but to minister'. If the people of God are to be truly the body of Christ, the servant of the world, then together Minister and people are called to 'minister'. I was convinced as I began my work at Central that this was the first priority for us all. If change was to come, then the vital motivating theme in our 'servanthood' must be the Christian concept of *love*. This was our 'theory' and there is 'nothing more practical than good theory'.

The Christ love, as I understand it, which is found in the New Testament, is a love that stimulates an inner drive to action; a love that propels persons into an immediate resolve to reach out with others in helpfulness, understanding, and forgiving service for the sake of others. At its best it is characterized by unlimited self-giving. It demonstrates its respect for other people seeking through service to make the 'servant' and the recipient of service—'whole'. The words of Jesus spell out this spirit of self-giving loud and clear. Jesus says 'whoever cares for his own safety is lost; but if a man will let himself be lost for My sake, he will find his true self'. (Matt. 16:25).

If the community of Christ is to mature, then its capacity for team-work, togetherness in service must grow. We only learn how to work with others, for others, when we seek how to achieve common positive goals. In seeking a Christian programme of helpfulness we are on the only road which leads to a sensible demonstration of what Christian discipleship means in the world. Such an approach creates a 'togetherness' which quickly generates the warm feelings of enthusiasm. But such love will be more than 'warm feelings' for it contains cool planning and calculation.

'The demand is to act where I am', as Rachel Handerlite once wrote, 'with others if possible for Christ's sake'. This understanding of love for other people is not abstract but specific, expressed in the performance of deeds by a team, as well as individual acts. We sought ways in which we could move forward along these lines. I saw my ministerial role in this as full time leader, there to initiate action, to encourage people to explore the way forward together, to help them to see how they could comfort one another in failure and re-create their vision and hope in worship. We have made a start!

**Into action**

If we were to lead then, the first hurdle was to attempt to get to know the individuals that comprised the congregation, and they to know my wife and myself. How could this be accomplished quickly? Of course we met people through our Sunday worship services and the inevitable handshaking ritual at the door of the church, but our real need was to break down the mass of outstretched hands and hurried smiles into individual persons. So we asked the Class Leaders if they would gather the members on their Class Books, plus adherents in their neighbourhood, into group meetings in their homes. We gave this project the title 'Getting to know you', which in itself explained the purpose of the meetings. In the first four months of our ministry in Preston, thirty-three groups were held in the homes and nearly 400 people attended. This enabled my wife and me to meet people face to face in the atmosphere of the home. Usually the gatherings lasted for an hour and a half. This project made it easier for us to put a name to a face, and to know something of the jobs and roles individual members of the congregation filled in the local community and in the church. The people began to feel that they knew a little about us. This project was only possible because of the willing co-operation of Leaders and people. Useful discussions ensued in every group. We began to feel acceptance by the church people. These meetings provided our first, tentative reconnaissance of the potential of the personnel within the church community. Out of this initial programme, with the advice of our deaconess and the counsel of our most experienced laymen, we asked the Leaders' Meeting to agree to the setting up of two work-parties, one on Sunday Worship and the other on Community Service. They have met at irregular intervals throughout the year. A brief summary of their terms of reference is as follows:

**Work Party on Worship**

1. To explore what can be done to make worship relevant to people's real needs and open up new methods of communication in Christian Worship.

2. To clarify aims and motives in undertaking experimental services and determine what it is hoped to achieve through them.

3. To see if there are ways in which we can involve people in the planning and preparation of Worship Services.

4. To gather information regarding any experiments in Worship which have been tried in other places.

5. To undertake some definite experiments in worship in the future at our church.

6. To set about evaluating experimental services so that we can make true judgments on the experiment.

7. To report to the Leaders' Meeting.

**Work Party on Community Service**

To give leadership in all matters affecting the social welfare of people within and beyond the church family. To enable the church to exercise a ministry of service in the community.

1. To seek new ways in which we can respond as Christians to human need.

2. To initiate ways of helping those in need.

3. Act as liaison with the town's Social Services and Voluntary Services.

4. To call on such people or organizations as it may be necessary for the adequate performance of such functions.

5. To report regularly to the Leaders' Meeting.

We did not look upon these Terms of Reference as final but rather as a starting point for action.

During the year useful attempts have been made in experiments in Worship under the initiative of this group. We decided to experiment in Worship to minister to some important sectors of our community in response to tentative overtures from them to us. Worship Services were arranged with the active co-operation of the following groups, Senior Citizens, Police, Nurses and Youth. These were very well supported by the people in these sectors of our community and highly valued by them.

The first of these experiments involved a tremendous effort in organizing transport. The Social Service Work Party handled this with great efficiency. All the Senior Citizens Clubs and organizations were contacted and large numbers of our elderly citizens shared in worship together at Central. The whole Worship Service was planned and directed to their special needs. Senior Citizens took part and formed the choir. Previous planning and participation in a Service for the Preston Constabulary was the hallmark of a most successful event, when Civic dignatories were present along with the Chief Constable and Watch Committee. This service was planned not so much to offer detailed solutions to specific problems faced by the police, as to focus Christian principles on which any solution to problems arising in police work could rest.

The nurses of Preston and District, led by their administrative officers were also engaged in a service designed to open up a discussion about Christianity and health. Nurses took part in the service, chose their own hymns and, standing, publicly re-affirmed their pledge, before the whole congregation, to the ministry of nursing.

After each of these Services of Worship, opportunity for light refreshments and informal meeting with members of the church was afforded in our coffee bar. Such contacts over a cup of tea or coffee, we regarded as a very important part of the exercise.

The Youth Worship Service was more venturesome still. The normal sermon was replaced by a dramatic modern re-enactment of the parable of 'The Good Samaritan' in the church, under the title of 'Thirty-nine Witnesses'. A special raised platform on various levels was erected for this experiment in contemporary worship, the scene being set in a New York street. These efforts directed to certain specific sectors in our community made an important start to build the bridge between contemporary society and the Church. These services were an opportunity to create a meeting point between church members and others.

The Social Service Work Party has been involved in attempts to enlarge the church's opportunities of Christian service pinpointing certain specific needs where we could be of help. The SOS Anonymous Telephone Service at Central pioneered by the previous minister was seen by him as a link between people in trouble and the ministry. This has been enlarged from a 'one man show' to include sixteen others who have made themselves available on a rota to help, where possible, people in need. Often the primary help they can give is simply to listen to the story of those who seek help. Through the initiative of our Group the whole scheme is to be enlarged into the 'Telephone Samaritan Service'. By encouraging the Council of Churches to come in, and others interested, whether they have a church affiliation or not, we expect our SOS volunteer helpers to be fully integrated with this national organization. This has involved a lot of patient negotiation with other churches through the Council and also with town authorities.

Another venture encouraged by this Work Party has been the setting up of a Rest Centre for the families of men in our local prison. This venture began in the autumn of 1969. Many wives and children make long journeys on Sunday to visit their relatives in prison. Often after the visiting time is over they simply wander round the streets of Preston awaiting buses or trains. Sometimes they get very wet in heavy rain. So it has been decided that for two hours each Sunday afternoon a Rest Centre should be opened in our Coffee Bar. This scheme is to be undertaken in full partnership and co-operation with the Probation After-care Service. A roster of people have volunteered for this useful piece of Christian service.

Under Christian Stewardship thirty-five church visitors committed to visit every church family once a quarter have now been formed into a Pastoral Committee. They meet once a quarter for discussion, the exchange of experiences, report and instruction which we hope will help them to be more effective in their important work. This quarterly meeting we regard as a very important development helping to express the pastoral care of the church through lay-folk and minister alike, for others.

Yet another group, comprising only five people, have been engaged together in producing a new quarterly magazine, *In Action*. The local Grammar School sixth form ran a competition to design the cover, the Careers Master undertook to be Editor, a local printing manager agreed to be head of production. The group was formed. The result was a lively, topical review, modern and up-to-date. The magazine, which is directed not only at church members but, we believe, will be of interest to non-churchgoers as well, replaces a smaller church-orientated publication. We see the present effort as a tool of the Mission. Already copies appear in the Reference Library and other Libraries, in the waiting room of Preston Station, school libraries, dentist and doctors' reception rooms and, of course, in the homes of all our people, and, we hope, their friends. Besides news and other features of interest, this quarterly attempts to give a Christian commentary on some contemporary events. We hope it will provoke debate and discussion on important issues of interest to Christians and non-Christians alike.

## Creative encounter

These are the first new tentative steps in our church programme to increasingly develop a creative encounter between the Church and the world. We are attempting to serve the society in which we are set where, perhaps, through personal contact and lively debate we can communicate our faith or provide a service without strings. One example from a number will suffice. We are welcoming the

Annual Meeting of the new Preston Council for Community Relations to our church this year. This is an important body seeking to promote racial harmony in our town between the coloured and white communities, attempting to iron out problems and difficulties as they arise. This is a body on which I now serve. The meeting attended by local members of Parliament met in the chapel itself—a fitting place, I think, for a town debate and the transaction of such essential work.

An article such as this can only sketch in some of the more important approaches in our long term endeavour to encourage the people of God *to be the people of God in this place*. For these tasks we all need training, the pooling of insight, the sharing of experience. Such an opportunity has been provided because of the generous financial response of Central's Leaders, and the support of the District. During the last six months two Lay Training Courses, under the leadership of the Lay Training Officer for the Methodist Church in the North West, have been undertaken at weekly meetings. The subjects under debate have been under two headings. Series (1) 'The Church in the Modern World' and Series (2) 'Aspects of the Mission of the Church today'. These courses have been an honest and realistic attempt to estimate the Church today, without cutting the nerve of moral effort, by assuming, as some would suggest, that reconstruction of the Church in Mission is hopeless. Methodist and non-Methodist have shared in this project in Christian education. We expect further developments on these lines in the future, as we open up opportunities for intelligent consideration of the task of the Church today. A Central church such as Lune Street can provide a service to a wide constituency by opening its doors to specific 'group-learning' projects like these under the Lay Training Officer.

### The way to mature

So much of Church life today is like 'plankton'—a Greek word meaning 'wandering', 'drifting'—an accurate term to describe much in the present church scene. There has been a loss of mission and of hope in so many places. Ultimately this is a judgement upon those of us who are committed to Christ and his Church. It is due to a failure of nerve, a loss of confidence. Confidence and hope will only be regained if we re-discover and, in a variety of ways, express our true humanity in Christian selfgiving service for others. We shall only mature as people when we seek a purposeful discipline, within a group committed to common goals. The fellowship of the Church needs to re-discover how each can participate at some point in a continuing purpose of serving others for Christ's sake. Perhaps if we can begin now to think out with others how we can act as disciples of Christ in the world, we shall find some points of contact, some way to express exciting Christian service.

Let us locate the need, then try to meet it where we can. We shall learn as we go. Our confidence will grow. As we attempt to serve human need, we shall become more adaptable, constructive, resourceful and respected. We shall make mistakes, sometimes fail, then we shall comfort each other, privately licking our wounds. As we work together we shall learn a new respect for those who share with us our high purposes. As a matter of fact, we shall begin to mature in mutual personal growth as disciples of Christ. Perhaps we shall also gain a clearer insight into what it means to be a Servant Church. Time alone will tell.

# 10. The English/Welsh Border Commission

**In 1961 the Methodist Conference, through the Home Mission Department, established a mobile team of ministers and deaconesses to work with twenty predominantly rural circuits which were in desperate plight in the Border country.**

'T A K E a problem situation, add a few extra staff, stir in some financial support and set the pot boiling.' So the cynic sums up the Methodist formula for success. He will go on to prophesy that when the 'heat' is turned off, the basic problems will float to the surface again leaving the chief cooks and bottle washers little wiser but significantly poorer.

Not a few made such a judgement on the Border experiment. Up to a point, there is a measure of truth which cannot be refuted. Eight years, incalculable man-hours, and £20,500 (the cost 1962–1968) later, and the bulk of the chapels on the English/Welsh Border are still plodding reluctantly towards their demise. Rankled by radicalism, disturbed by desecration of the Sabbath, licking wounds from trials of strength, the minority groups of the conservative evangelicals are glad to see the back of the core team and wait for the dispersal of the wider team. But some factors have emerged of positive significance.

The experiment in rural mission began with the three Methodist Districts who had an oversight of the area. Under the guidance of the Home Mission Department, they undertook a careful survey of this depleted, struggling part of the Church. The subsequent annual Conference (1961) approved the organization of the Border Commission: a team leader (the Revd Ronald P. Marshall) with assistant ministers and deaconesses were appointed with an open brief for missioning the twenty circuits. This team varied in membership through the years, its maximum strength being seven full time workers.

The tactics of this core team were to share with local circuits in a wide variety of enterprise. Remembering the unequivocal success of the first Home Mission caravans in previous years, it seems that among those who conceived the scheme and those who welcomed it at the grass roots, there was a strong expectation of a massive permutation of caravan-mission techniques. Happily, the team planned otherwise. They sought to explore such avenues as youth conferences, lay training, Christian stewardship and so on.

It took four years from the inception of the Border Commission to unearth the most constructive strategy. The superintendents of the circuits involved, persuaded by the core team, agreed to set up four regionally based work parties to study respectively, the use of Sunday in mission, youth work, lay leaders training, and group methods. The reports from the four groups were drawn together to form a policy paper under the title, 'Thinking Things Through Together'.

The publication of this booklet for the Border Circuits initiated a chain reaction of work parties and experiments. Some circuits tackled the whole report, some undertook detailed study of a part of it, others were inspired to launch out on an associated concern for mission. Whatever happens in the Border area, the 'work-party method' will find a continuing use as it calls ministers and laymen to share policy-formation and practical evangelism together. It is highly unlikely that this method would have been so well informed without all the background research, co-ordinating endeavour and personal contribution of the core team.

There is no need to go fully into the details of the whole history of the Border Commission because it is amply recounted in *Border Experiment* (Home Mission Department, 1968, 6s.). Some points can, however, be made for future consideration as the dust begins to settle after the termination of the mobile-core-team contribution.

1. The principle of using a fully mobile core team was wholly vindicated. Being a participant in the experiment one is able to acknowledge the valuable stimulus afforded by them: they were able to share their privilege of wider perspectives with local ministers and laymen who are so often cribbed and confined by circuit boundaries. Moreover, the advantage of someone with specialized ability operating over a wider field than a local circuit affords was clearly discernable.

2. The area chosen was far too large for significant cohesion in a common identity of purpose. The area, one hundred and twenty-five miles from one end to the other, up to forty miles in width,

serviced by very poor roads, presented a formidable, indeed impossible, territory to manage. Any similar undertaking should take account of factors other than mutual desperation. The sociological word finding fashion and of which we need to take account is 'the Zone'. This means that in addition to the marathon of miles to be encountered, there were pre-existent socially derived tensions which inevitably conflicted with a sense of cohesion so desirable for this kind of venture.

3. These two points converge to suggest the possibility for an experiment in rural areas involving a 'federation of circuits'. In this we would envisage a common policy of mission undertaken by joint planning of circuits within a zone. A redeployment of the ministry could release two or three full time workers with specialized ministries through the entire area. First considered for the Hereford area, plans are proceeding more favourably around Ludlow and its environs.

4. The Border experiment became, though I doubt it was an intention in the beginning, a 'test-bed' for basic prototypes of mission ventures. The religious life of the area was at a low ebb with microcosmic communities of Methodists, predominantly elderly and short of competent and virile lay leadership. Thus when a particular experiment is deemed a failure, here it might possibly be that not the method but the inadequacy of the situation is at fault. There would be real justification in using this type of experiment in a 'stronger area' in order to learn lessons for rural work.

5. It is perhaps a widely acknowledged fact—but it is worth repeating what we learned experientially—that the renewal of the Church is not simply a matter of discovering the right techniques. The fundamental demand is for the rediscovery of a credible understanding of God, an authentic expression of Christian community and a 'new mutation of Christian' (John Vincent). Only in such an environment of patent credibility can techniques be so important.

6. I feel that a distinct lesson has to be learned from the transition of the Border Experiment into its second phase. In September 1968, the full-time core team was finally withdrawn. Undoubtedly the Home Mission Department were right in adopting the attitude that an experiment cannot go on for ever. But were the decisions they made ones which were likely to ensure that the project was thoroughly completed? They appointed a part-time secretary to the Commission who is a minister in a Border circuit, reconstituted the Commission to comprise all the superintendent ministers and cir-

cuit stewards from the twenty circuits, and sought to devolve the responsibility back upon the circuits.

No doubt the amount of money available for continuing the experiment was limited. The area has benefited from generous Home Mission support over many years and more so during the existence of the Border Commission—no one can belittle this. Nevertheless, the concluding stages of an experiment are at least as important as the process of experimentation. The cost—in all senses—should have been calculated before the structure was built.

The appointed part-time secretary has to carry the mantle of the former full-time leader of the core team: he has been allotted an impossible task. Though he is applying himself with commendable energy and enthusiasm, he is inevitably reduced to the capacity of 'administrative secretary' over an area he can scarcely expect to cover with any regularity let alone depth. His opportunities for a ministry which evokes fresh endeavour from local circuits is severely limited by such elementary facts as that there are only twenty-four hours in a day. To presume that no further stimulus is necessary on the Border is to misread its needs.

The valued supportive and creative role of carefully chosen ministers and laymen through the Border Commission Committee has been dissipated by replacing them with eighty local circuit officials. When they are brought together for a short day conference, such a body does not expect to achieve too many great objectives.

While the devolution of responsibility on to circuits has an admirable facet of realism, it is finally a disastrous surrender to the entrenched forces of parochial conservatism. Practical experience assures us of the catalyst quality of partly external bodies.

Because of these dilutions to the Border Commission programme, policy, and personnel, there is little wonder that popular opinion believes—despite circulars to the contrary—that the Border experiment ended in September 1968.

7. In retrospect, the report and evaluation published has at least one severe limitation. The Commission, which reported to Conference in 1961, had undertaken a vast amount of research into the state of the work along the Border. Many facts were recorded statistically; their interpretation gave a picture of the churches on the Border; the character and quality of circuit life was laid bare. Should not the same analysis have been made *after* the first phase of the experiment? Such an evaluation and comparison with the previous inquiry may have displayed many unpleasant truths for those of us in the local situation, but it would have been invaluable

in assessing the worthwhileness of the expenditure and determining policy for the future.

8. The report and evaluation, with what limitations it contains, has had a wide circulation. One would have anticipated, however, that in the Border, particularly in the Border Commission Committee, it would have been treated mercilessly in cross-examination: almost as the Cabinet examines a white paper. We have made no pretentious claims for its verbal inspiration: in many ways it is a document valid for only a period of time; but it purports to be the evaluation of the experiment which has been a considerable item of Church expenditure if nothing else. The only collective consideration in the context of the Border Commission that I recall is an hours 'discussion' with sixty people present. The basic question has still not been put: 'Is this evaluation sufficiently valid for us to draw conclusions about the next positive step?' Mission can only be truly experimental if the results of one experiment become the basis for the next. Should this kind of experiment, with appropriate adjustments, be applied elsewhere? It is still not too late to answer.

# 11. Grove Hill Social Enquiry

## REPORT FROM MIDDLESBROUGH COUNCIL OF CHURCHES

### Introduction

A JOINT committee of the Social Responsibility Group of the Middlesbrough Council of Churches and the Christian Citizenship Committee of the Methodist Church in Middlesbrough were concerned to know if there were unmet needs in Middlesbrough which the Churches could help meet. This report describes how this concern was acted upon in 1967–8 and an appraisal of the results of that action.

### Summary

A series of public meetings were held in which church members, social workers and clergy met with local inhabitants of the Grove Hill Area and observers from other parts of Middlesbrough. From these meetings a list of specific tasks of supportive help was compiled and a system of directing available resources to meet these needs was devised and set up and is now functioning in that area.

### Method

*Stage 1.* The joint committee of the Social Responsibility Group of the Middlesbrough Council of Churches and the Christian Citizenship Committee of the Methodist Church in Middlesbrough set up a small working party to study the problem and advise the parent committee of the most appropriate course of action.

The working party studied other similar ventures, which had been reported, and discussed ways and means of achieving the objective in Middlesbrough.

It was agreed that it would be best to run a pilot scheme anchored to a particular discreet area in Middlesbrough and study that area in depth.

In consultation with the Heads of Departments of the Statutory Social Services it was agreed that Grove Hill would be a suitable compact area of appropriate size and opportunity.

*Stage 2.* The working party then sought the active co-operation of the clergy of the area. The local clergy readily accepted the involvement even to the extent of taking on the brunt of the work of organizing the project and providing the nucleus around which further work would evolve.

Representatives of the working party and the local clergy were given an opportunity to explain the project to an existent Grove Hill Social Workers' Luncheon Club. The help and advice provided by this club was very valuable and encouraging and some of the members subsequently took part in panels and group sessions.

It was agreed at this stage that the project should take the form of a series of about half a dozen public meetings, to be held on completely 'neutral' ground at the Grove Hill Community Centre.

*Stage 3.* The next stage involved a considerable amount of planning, arranging and contacting of speakers and this phase was undertaken by a committee composed of the original working party, the nucleus of clergy in the Grove Hill Area and one or two co-opted members.

This committee met regularly until the programme of meetings and speakers was provisionally arranged.

The objectives of the next stage of the project were agreed to be as follows:

(*a*) Through open public meetings to conduct an enquiry into the extent of social need in the Grove Hill area and thereafter to try to meet such of the unmet need as the resources available can meet.

(*b*) To advise in the longer term what steps should be taken to meet needs in other parts of Middlesbrough.

The open public meetings should be addressed by a panel of social workers who would each speak for about ten minutes of the needs in the Grove Hill Area as they saw them, the services that each was able to offer and the extent to which voluntary part time help could be used to support them in meeting outstanding unmet need.

The meetings should then divide into groups who would discuss the substance of what is revealed by the panel and come forward with their ideas and questions in a plenary session which would be taken down by a scribe.

These reports would then be presented at the sixth meeting when agreement would be sought on specific tasks which could be undertaken by unskilled voluntary part time resources, particularly the Churches in the area.

It would be decided in the light of the situation at that meeting when agreement would be sought on specific tasks which could be undertaken by unskilled voluntary part time resources, particularly the Churches in the area.

It would be decided in the light of the situation at that meeting what should be the next step.

The plans were put and explained to the joint meeting of the Social Responsibility Group of the Council of Churches and the Christian Citizenship Committee and were agreed.

*Stage 4.* A programme and introduction was used as the main medium of publicity. Copies were distributed to all involved and to the members of the Council of Churches. In addition copies were put into every house in the area and announcements were made in pulpits, and posters were put in local shops, libraries, the Community Centre and church notice boards.

After the first meeting the Press were given a report which was given mention in the local newspaper.

*Stage 5.* The meetings were arranged as follows:

(a) *Introduction.* In which the general background of the area was described by a local councillor, a general practitioner, a policeman, a housing officer and a local housewife.

(b) *Family needs.* In which the panel consisting of a junior school head, a health visitor, a Children's Department worker, a school welfare officer discussed family needs.

(c) *Family needs.* In which the panel consisting of a housing officer, a welfare worker, a Children's Department worker, and an officer of the NSPCC discussed families in greater need.

(d) *Teenagers.* In which the panel consisting of a youth employment officer, a probation officer, a policewoman, a senior school teacher, a youth club leader, discussed the needs of young people.

(e) *Handicapped, Housebound and Sick.* In which a welfare worker, a psychiatric social worker, a matron of an Old People's Home, the WRVS and a general practitioner discussed the needs of the physically and mentally sick and hospitalised or housebound.

(*f*) *Where now*. In which a presentation was made of the findings of the previous meetings using visual aids, and agreement was reached on what should be done next.

*Stage 6*. (*a*) It was agreed that there were a number of simple tasks of short duration which could be performed by people who had time and concern which would both meet needs which were at present not met, or would release trained social workers to use their skills rather than being forced to use their time on relatively unskilled work which could be performed by willing neighbourly people.

(*b*) It was agreed that there are many services available to those in need which are not effectively communicated to them. It was decided therefore that a pamphlet outlining the services available should be put into every house in the Grove Hill Area.

(*c*) It was agreed that a system should be set up to bring together the resources and those who need them. An Action Group was set up to act as a clearing house for requests for help and advice. The Community Centre Warden would be the liaison officer because there was a manned telephone at the Grove Hill Community Centre. Any requests for help should be passed by individuals or by social workers to the Warden who would then pass on the request to the appropriate person or service.

The group would then meet once each month to check progress on the list of requests for help and feed in any new ones to the system.

(*d*) Any needs which required more than individual help would be pursued along the appropriate channels by the group.

*Stage 7*. (*a*) When the Action Group met it decided that it should adopt the name and symbol AID to identify its activities.

(*b*) The members came to the second meeting with a measure of the resources they could each commit from the groups or churches they represented.

(*c*) Once an estimate had been made of the resources available a statement was made to the Press describing the nature of the Enquiry, the findings and the intended action and some good publicity was gained.

(*d*) Up to now about thirty individual requests for help have been met in addition to regular visitation at local old people's homes, and help with work at the Community Centre on behalf of Old People.

(*e*) The requests so far have been mainly for visitation, shopping, gardening, decorating and domestic chores.

*Stage 8*. (*a*) In the next week or two a pamphlet will be issued to every house in Grove Hill and simultaneously there will be Press coverage which is expected to bring forward more requests for help.

(*b*) All the social services will be notified of what is being done so that requests can be directed to the appropriate service or the AID committee for attention.

(*c*) A form will be issued to Church and other group members on which they can commit themselves to a specific number of hours per week or month and can choose the sorts of tasks they would be able to undertake.

## Appraisal

As this was a pilot scheme the following points are made in retrospect to help others who might contemplate a similar venture.

(*a*) A project of this nature takes about two years and there are stages of high activity and stages of slow or low activity. Because of this there should be some means of maintaining cohesion among the participants of the action group throughout this period. It is suggested that the group should have a *raison d'être* over and above this project. The ideas that suggest themselves are of a study group on religious sociology, or PND group, or a programmed series of dialogues between the group and individual social workers in the area.

(*b*) There are considerable advantages to be gained by having an existing nucleus of local ecumenical co-operation on which to build such a venture.

(*c*) If public meetings are held there is a need for detailed planning of each meeting with the participants to ensure each knows his role and is provided with any visual aids which will assist him in presenting his material concisely, clearly and graphically.

(*d*) The chairman for a public meeting should be chosen for his skill and not position. He, above all, should be carefully primed and prepared.

(*e*) It should be made clear at every stage what proportion of the participants and attenders at meetings are indigenous and what proportion are observers from other areas.

(*f*) It cannot be assumed that one area has the same needs as another.

(*g*) There is a need for strong and continuous leadership by one person who can commit himself to the project for a period of two or three years even if some of the committee members change from time to time.

(*h*) Some form of commitment procedure for resources should be established before the where now stage. There should be no pressure put on anyone to commit themselves but an opportunity should be provided on a form which they can sign.

## Conclusions

1. There is unmet need in Middlesbrough and there are untapped resources available to meet some of that need.

2. There is a considerable communication gap between those in need and those able to meet the need.

3. The Church in the local situation can help provide a bridge between the two if it is prepared to lose its identity in co-operation with others who are concerned to help meet need.

4. The Church in the local situation must work ecumenically to gain acceptance by those others who seek support in the valuable work they already do for those they know are in need.

5. The Church can release the skilled caseworker for fuller Stewardship of their skills by undertaking a caring supportive role requiring more practical skills.

6. The Churches should make it clear, albeit not too overtly, that they do not seek self-advertisement or recruitment from their participation in such ventures.

7. It is recommended that existing local ecumenical groups in Middlesbrough explore the possibility of co-operating with social workers and other socially conscious groups in their own area to discover the most effective ways of meeting the needs which they find there.

8. It is recommended that they become involved together in discovering the nature and extent of the need because it is this process which encourages commitment and not merely the reading of a report or set of statistics.

9. It is recommended that the Council of Churches make itself aware of any similar experiments, enterprises, studies or project going on in Middlesbrough to ensure that work is not duplicated and to ensure that the Church has an opportunity to co-operate in such work.

10. It is recommended that in areas where there is not already active ecumenical co-operation some, even loosely formed, groups be fostered in preparation for local action at some future date.

**A Summary of results outlining some of the needs in the Grove Hill area**

AGED

*a.* Help from the family where possible.
*b.* Good neighbour service; help with chores; help with shopping; help with transport; helping by combating loneliness, sit and chat; regular visits to check that all is well.
*c.* Assistance with the meals on wheels service.
*d.* Clinics for old people; as for children.
*e.* Help from public for old people resident in Old People's Homes:

(i) Accompanying the residents on hospital dental and optical appointments (with or without transport)
(ii) Visitors for those who have no relatives or regular visitors.
(iii) People who will take residents out to tea.
(iv) People who will take residents to libraries.
(v) People who will arrange outings.
(vi) People who will organize shows and concerts.
(vii) Children who will go and visit as a party from schools, etc.
(viii) People willing to help residents with hobbies and handicrafts.

PHYSICALLY HANDICAPPED

*a.* Provide transport.
*b.* Provide time for pushing wheel chairs.
*c.* Provide warning light schemes.
*d.* Arrange parties and outings.

HOSPITALIZED AND MENTALLY HANDICAPPED

*a.* Assistance with occasional transport to free the ambulance service for more urgent work.
*b.* Kindly people who will visit those in phobic anxiety states and accompany them to the shops, etc.
*c.* Assistance with beauty culture and general hygiene.
*d.* Hospital visitation and library work.
*e.* Friends and neighbours who will see to it that patients at home take their prescribed medications.

YOUNG PEOPLE

*a.* Any apparent immorality involving young girls should be reported.
*b.* Need for more provision for 11–14 years olds.
*c.* Need for informal facilities such as coffee bars and discotheques to be provided by the new Teesside Authority.
*d.* Help in providing jobs for handicapped young people.
*e.* Need for good homes to accept and help children from bad homes.
*f.* Need for support and guidance from home and school.
*g.* Need for young people to be helped to make a contribution to meeting needs.
*h.* Need for dances and dance tuition.

GENERAL

*a.* Need for more supportive help for problem families.
*b.* Need for links between those who are in need and those who can meet the needs.
*c.* Ways of communicating to those in need what facilities already exist.
*d.* The need for more resources.
*e.* Need for pressure group to get more social workers.
*f.* Need to be aware and concerned at administrative inefficiencies.
*g.* Need for a community spirit.
*h.* Need for local officials to be known in the area.
*i.* A more enlightened policy with respect to placement of tenants by the Housing Officers.
*j.* Need for more facilities for children.
*k.* Need to insist on conditions of tenancy being upheld.
*l.* Need for modernization of housing interior.
*m.* Leadership is needed from the Youth.
*n.* The entry age for the Community Centre should be reduced from 18–14 years.
*o.* A Youth Centre should be provided near the Community Centre.

# 12. Communicare House, Killingworth

## NEWCASTLE UPON TYNE

### 1. Killingworth

A N overspill town, officially called Killingworth Township, on the northern fringe of Tyneside. Population is expected to be some 20,000 by 1975. Employment will be on Tyneside and in offices and factories in the Township. Planning and development is by the Northumberland County Council which employs a professional team under Mr R. G. A. Gazzard as Director of Development. The planners are keeping their responsibility for the creation of a new community very much in mind, far more than just planting buildings.

### 2. The Experimenters

The Social Services Committee for Killingworth, representing those particulary concerned with the care of the people of Killingworth, both the present population and all those who will come in the future. Both Statutory and Voluntary bodies are represented.

More particularly the Killingworth Christian Council which represents the Anglican, Methodist, Roman Catholic and Presbyterian Churches. To a large extent the Council has become the agent of the Social Services Committee in the setting up and conduct of the experiment. The Council also conducts experiments in its own right. The Council is a registered charity.

### 3. The Needs

By 31 December 1968, some 2,500 had moved into Killingworth. Development is still at a fairly early stage therefore but it is at this time that the seeds of the future success of the town are sown— whether it will be a place in which the residents can take a pride and in which they will be glad to bring up their children, or not. Mr Gazzard and his team are well aware of this and the Social Services Committee was formed long before the first house was occupied. A Community Association was also formed, before there were a hundred houses occupied, and the Christian Council, drawn of necessity from those in the surrounding areas at first, rather than Killingworth residents, came into being at much the same time.

We all took note of the Ministry of Housing pamphlet 'The First Hundred Houses' and wished to implement its recommendation of temporary premises for community use at a very early stage in a town's development. We also noted that the pamphlet states that no funds are available for such a purpose.

Throughout 1966 various ways by which such premises might be provided were explored. These included the conversion of some existing farm buildings and the construction of prefabricated buildings. Finally we found that the best practicable solution was that one of the new houses should be rented and we are grateful to the housing authority for making this possible.

## 4. Communicare House

So in January 1967, the first Communicare House opened and provided for the following needs which seemed to be paramount at this stage:

*a. A person* living in the house—the Warden. A trained Anglican Church Worker was recruited and she has been very fully used in a great variety of ways, some trivial but many reaching towards people at a time of great need. By the fact of being there, in a place to which a considerable proportion of the population finds its way for some purpose or another, she has become the best known person in Killingworth, someone to whom those who 'have no-one to turn to' can go and find an open door and listening ear.

For the newly established community has little of the support from the 'extended family' and long-standing near neighbours that exists in the old inner city parts from which most residents come. (But good-neighbourliness has from the start been a feature of Killingworth, helped by the layout of the houses around intimate courts along, or off, the pedestrian-way system.)

*b. Room for a Doctor* to practice, very limited in the first Communicare House, it was in fact the kitchen hurriedly adapted for each Surgery hour. In the second house the Doctor has his own room on the first floor; it was largely in order to obtain this that the move was made. A daily Surgery is held, on four days at mid-day, on the remaining two in the evening. Prescriptions are delivered daily by a Chemist.

For one of the earliest needs expressed was for a Doctor.

*c. Space for an Infant Welfare Clinic.* Needing, and using, the same facilities as the Doctor, though at different hours of course.

For, in common with all similar developments, there is a disproportionate number of small children compared with the country as a whole and the birth-rate is very high.

*d. Meeting facilities for groups of the population,* again very restricted on account of the space available, but Communicare House did provide the initial sole meeting place. More recently a school has become available. The House still caters for the smaller meetings, usually in the day-room downstairs.

For many people, but not all, feel the need of social comings-together. In a small house and with limited resources this must take place outside the home. The facilities of the big city must be reinforced by small scale local meeting places. The 'Local' provides this for men but not, in the North East anyway, for women and not for children and young people (who especially need shelter, warm, noise-proof if possible, where they can be secure both in their own minds and in the minds of their parents).

*e. Accommodation* for the Warden personally and for a companion. The Warden has the upstairs sitting room of this four bedroom house as a bed-sitter. A student lodger has her own room and there is a common room with some cooking facilities, used especially when events downstairs make the main kitchen unavailable. Another bedroom can be used for the occasional guest and for small meetings.

For the Warden's job, in the midst of all the bustle, can be a lonely one. Indeed some accommodation of this sort seems to be an important part of such a set-up and we would like to suggest to those responsible for the care of older 'teenagers that they might consider such multi-purpose set-ups regularly—neither a foster-home nor a hostel but something in between.

*f. Space needed by the Church.* Worship on a small scale and, at first, on a denominational basis started as soon as Communicare House opened. The Churches also used the house as a meeting point where township people could conveniently consult clergy and ministers. The Killingworth Christian Council meets in the house and Confirmation and other classes are held there.

For without the worship of God in Jesus Christ the experiment could not properly be termed a Christian one. It is not by exclusively human scheming that a quality of living and caring which is, even in the faintest measure, a reflection of that of Christ can be achieved but by open-ness to his Spirit—and that means prayer and worship.

*g. A demonstration of the Christian Gospel,* a visual aid in other words—the Church doing something, not just saying something. The house carries a label saying that it is the premises of the Killingworth Christian Council and in the visiting of newcomers, both by ecumenical lay teams and by the Warden, this point is made. Nevertheless the house is commonly taken for granted and the Churches' part in it not understood.

For it is surely consistent with the Gospel that premises provided by the Church should, especially in a new area where anything other than houses is a rare asset, serve not just the small community of those who wish to attend Church but the whole community.

## 5. The Communicare principle

So far as the Christian Council knows the term 'Communicare' was first used in proposals put forward by Dr Jeavons in connection with the development of Tile Cross, Birmingham. He likened the family in trouble to a badly addressed parcel directed and redirected from one agency to another in search of the right slot. The principle is endorsed in the Seebohm Report.

In any case of more than trivial trouble it is the whole family that is involved, not solely the individual immediately afflicted. This is recognized when, for example, a newly widowed mother informs her child's school of the death of its father, knowing that the school will recognize that special consideration may be needed for a time. Serious accident or sickness, whether to the wage-earner or to the housewife, will raise problems that will involve not only Doctor and hospital, employer and MOSS but any one or more of the Children's Department, Labour Exchange, School Attendance Officer and even the local library.

Any form of serious trouble is likely to be psycho-somatic in its effects. Depression will be expressed to a Doctor in terms most likely to arouse his concern—'Doctor, I get frequent headaches' when 'Doctor, I need someone to talk to' might be more to the point.

A coronary may be the result of tension at work or tension at home and may produce feelings of guilt in the other partner in a marriage. So may a death.

Someone to talk to, feelings of guilt, are, or should be, within the sphere of the Clergy but unless a Clergyman/Minister/Priest is already known and appreciated those in need will probably not easily make the necessary contact, nor open up if contact is made. There are considerations here relevant to Clergy training and further-training.

The concept of 'Communicare' is relevant not only to the general public in search of help but also to the helpers themselves. Necessary specialization by workers must not mean a tendency to categorize cases as either exclusively within their own sphere or, on the other hand, exclusively outside it. It has not been unknown for a Children's Officer, a Probation Officer, a School Attendance Officer and perhaps a Moral Welfare Worker all to be visiting the same family unbeknown to each other. Commonly, today, and this takes place in Killingworth, in Communicare House, informal meetings, often over lunch, provide contacts which makes the integration of care easier.

In stable communities a great deal of the caring for a family in trouble is done in the first place by relatives living close by. Neighbours support each other and unsophisticated though such help may be it is kindly and, emanating from intimate personal knowledge and a shared background, goes a very long way. In other words even today such communities as pit villages are in a very real measure self-supportive.

On the other hand in a new community two factors operate which necessitate a much greater degree of outside support:

*a.* The youthfulness of the community means that it is particularly vulnerable in that range of troubles involving children and, by the same factor, a shortage of the older generation means a lack of those free to help in emergency. So there are more emergencies and less help immediately available to meet them.

*b.* The absence of relatives and friends of long standing and a reluctance to involve comparative strangers in one's own troubles. (Though experience shows that once the message has got through that there is an emergency on, help is forthcoming in generous measure.)

## 6. The Church's part in Communicare

The minister (to use a term intended to cover trained workers of all denominations, ordained and lay, male and female) will be the spearhead of the work of the organized Church in any community. This is not to deny that a Christian in any specialized agency working for the care of the community, or indeed a Christian in any worth-while occupation, does not do it 'in the name of Christ', but the minister is popularly held to represent the organized Church, if not Christ personally. His 'image' however is too often presented as of bungling, if well meaning, amateurism. Like any other profession, today he has to earn respect, he cannot assume it automatically. This is one reason why the three year stint of many ministers is quite inappropriate in this situation.

The minister who is a member of the Communicare team can contribute, firstly, in regard to those to whom their Christianity is a vital part of their way of life. They will expect his ministry at a time of emergency and it may often be relevant to workers in other spheres to know of this facet in the life of one they are trying to help. It should be relevant, for example, in a case of terminal illness to know that those involved are mature Christians.

Secondly, in the case of the large number of people whose Christianity is merely nominal, who turn to religion only in emergency, the minister must be easily available in the emergency. It is not for him to despise such a Christianity but gladly to help a fellow human being in any way he can—without judging them. A minister will be informed of a death and be able to extend his pastoral care to the bereaved. A Street Warden scheme may inform him of other emergencies but day to day contact with workers in other fields in a Communicare Centre will extend both the range and the depth of the pastoral care available in the area. Again, the training, experience and maturity of the ministry is of critical importance if he is to earn the confidence of his lay colleagues in the Communicare team.

Finally, the Church should be able to give to a Communicare Centre a soul, that is to say a warmth and a depth that would combat any tendency to a coldly clinical approach. That a ministry of intercession can and should be a natural part of the Church's contribution is also obvious.

## 7. The theology of the experiment

It is assumed:

*a.* That God is active in Killingworth with or without the Church, or the Churches. Christians do not therefore 'possess' God as a benefit to bestow on others. God may choose to use Christians in Killingworth, in so far as they do not resist that choice of them and its implications. His use of us can be in a myriad of different ways but the New Testament, as well as subsequent Christian experience, seems to show that there will be the following characteristics:

that the Ministry of Jesus is the prototype
that its purpose and end is unity with God through Jesus Christ.
that its method of working is loving care, the agape, translated 'charity', of 1 Corinthians 13.

and therefore Christians participate and rejoice in any act of caring by any agency. And they must not do this, even so, with an assumption of any moral or spiritual superiority—for God can use anyone; it cannot be assumed that he works better through those who go to Church.

*b.* This results in the belief that there is no division between care of the soul and care of the body or mind. Jesus did not make any differentiation in his ministry but healed bodies and forgave sins, treating them as two aspects of the same action. Service to others, even very prosaic service, is the will of God *per se* and not merely as a bait to lure people into occupying pew space. Nevertheless, as has already been stated, such service is a demonstration of the Gospel and can be expected to be more effective than a purely verbal preaching.

*c.* After life itself human need is for food and shelter. Today Western man would add as his next need freedom from suffering. But in the biblical views this is not as important a need as peace with God. Jesus Christ, by accepting the discipline that love must have and, in the end, great suffering, has by his sonship of the Father and by his victory over the ultimate evil of death lifted man, in his own self, into unity with God—'God was in Christ reconciling the world to himself'. The making actual of this in the lives of individual men and in society in general must be the most fundamental human need of all, in Killingworth and everywhere else. This is to be achieved through discipleship of Jesus Christ. To the earliest Christians this discipleship was a personal one with a living visible Christ. It is basic to Christianity all down the centuries since that a comparable personal relationship can be experienced with the living but invisible Christ. Prayer and worship, therefore, are not the optional extras in the lives of certain whose hobby is religion, as many today view it, but fundamental to any full and satisfying human existence and any who neglect them are, not wicked, but deprived.

Heaven is not a place we go to when we've died if we've done well enough in this life but a state which we can start to enjoy here and now, a state which is permanent (or 'eternal') and a state which completely transcends environment and circumstances such that, as St. John teaches, the crucifixion of Christ was also his glorification. Evangelism, therefore, is not the process of whipping up support for the Church but the opening up by God of new life to men and to mankind.

*d.* Jesus's ministry led him to the cross. Loving and caring today, even in the faintest imitation of his way, does not, as we might at first think, automatically lead to admiration and popularity and Christians must neither aim for that nor expect it.

*e.* Ecumenical working is practically an accepted assumption in such conditions as a New Town presents. A New Town, and many another community in our land, is a missionary situation for the Church. These two facts go together. Only the visible unity of the Christian Church can satisfy our ambitions for two reasons:

Anything less is inconsistent with the Church's calling as the Body of Christ.

Anything less is quite ineffective in a missionary situation.

## 8. Assessment

After two years of the pilot experiment it is possible to make only a preliminary assessment. The house has been sufficiently well used to have made a move to a larger house, when it became available after about fifteen months, imperative. The Doctor especially pressed for this but the Warden, too, found the demands on her such that she had to have more space for her own use. In the second house, although there are more rooms in all there is none as big as the main room in the previous house. This has been compensated for by the permission to use school premises out of school hours (in the end an additional Caretaker was appointed by the Education Department to allow this).

The house has played its part both in general and medical welfare in the life of the Church. It is doubtful if a Doctor would be practising in the township yet, but for Communicare House being available. The Child Welfare Clinic, too, is well used. Whilst the Welfare Services have not drawn many people to the house there have been a number of occasions when their integration has been helped forward as a result of contacts made in the house, particularly in the regular Workers' Lunch, at first held weekly but now monthly. Children and 'teenagers have used the house fully, especially until the schools became more available for their use. At first the Warden had a very big hand in organizing youth activities, but the County has been able to take on more of this responsibility.

The Warden has a very demanding task and it is a measure of the success of the house, and of her own ministry in and from it, that this is so. It is very urgent that additional help should be found for the Parish in order that the Warden can concentrate entirely on the running of the house and her ministry to the contacts it gives her.

So far as worship is concerned, the Church has outgrown the house. There are two Roman Catholic Masses each Sunday in a Contractor's canteen. In the early days of the planning of Killingworth there was an agreement made by the remaining denominations that there should be at least a monthly joint evening service as soon as premises became available. However, when a school hall was about to become available, we came to realize that evening worship is sinking fast and was not likely to attract many in a new town. Evening worship would not have been in direct competition with neighbouring churches (the township site is largely surrounded by older built up areas). Morning worship, however, would mean the founding of a new congregation and if this was to be on a united basis it would be an ecumenical congregation. Not without fears and anxieties, and after consultation with Bishop, Superintendent, Presbytery, etc., we came to see that this was just what the situation demanded. At first, because of well known complications, this worship was non-sacramental, a form of the Ministry of the Word. This could not last and the desire for the sacrament became obvious. After further consultation with higher authorities in the denominations, a form of simultaneous celebration was permitted, using the Anglican Series 2 order and the Lectionary produced by the Joint Liturgical Group. An Anglican Priest and a Free Church Minister con-celebrate, if that is the right term, at these services. At present Communion is only monthly, this is not too frequent for those used to quarterly Communion and, in addition, those not used to going to Church at all may feel very much out of things if they are offered no alternative to the Communion service in which they feel they cannot yet fully participate.

The Church's pastoral ministry to the people of Killingworth has certainly been enhanced by the presence of the house and its Warden, both as a centre for activities and interviews and also because of the contacts that have been made there with workers in other fields.

## 9. The future

*a. The Communicare Centre.* The County Council propose to build a Centre for all the activities and facilities outlined above, as well as for such further provisions, especially in the field of sport and entertainment, as can be catered for. The Church is offered a place in this complicated building. To the County Council this will mean even fuller use of expensive facilities, especially at weekends. To the Church this will mean that initial capital cost will be very low, little more than the cost of those items of furniture which only the Church needs. The accommodation for the exclusive use of the Christian Council will be on a cost-lease basis. Shared space will be taken at an hourly rate. There will, of course, be a share of heat, light and maintenance to be paid as there would be if the Church owned its own premises. Apart from any financial advantage the Church will, in this way, continue to be involved in the integrated care of the community in all its aspects. The Christian Council has asked for the sole use of:

A chapel to seat twenty-five to fifty.
A Vestry/Interview room with storage space.
An office.
A Counselling room for clergy studies.
Additional storage space for children's work.

The Council would like the occasional use of:

Space for some 300 people to worship in, including a foyer with serving facilities.
Catering facilities.
A Lounge/Committee Room.
Further committee rooms.

Adequate storage space for chairs.
Toilets, of course.

(further details can be found in the brief obtainable from Communicare House).

The Roman Catholic Church expects to provide its own worshipping space but to share the rest of the facilities. It would be very good if this RC Church could be built attached to the Communicare Centre.

*b. The Christian Council.* Negotiations are proceeding for the recognition of Killingworth as an 'Area of Ecumenical Experiment', after the pattern proposed at the Nottingham Faith and Order Conference. It is very important that there should be good lines of communication between those working and/or living in Killingworth and the higher formations of the denominations, otherwise there is a danger of the experiment becoming a purely local aberration leading to a new peculiar sect of Killingworth Christians.

*c. An ecumenical team ministry.* At this stage it is possible to do little more than mention that the founding of such a team is a very important part of the task facing the Christian Council in the next twelve months or so. So far all ministers working at all in Killingworth have responsibilities in other places as well—full time involvement in Killingworth is bound to grow with the population.

# 13. Consultations at Whirlow Grange

SINCE 1954 Whirlow Grange, the conference house of the Diocese of Sheffield, has been in regular use as a centre for lay education. In the early days this took the form of 'lay training courses', each involving three long week-ends, with membership recruited direct from the parishes. These courses did an immense amount of good in producing progressive informed lay leadership in certain parishes and a team of keen laymen ready to give a lead in church renewal throughout the diocese. Their very success, however, led to the request that they should be supplemented by 'consultations' of a more specialist nature to which people should be invited because they were members of a particular trade or profession, because they were engaged in a particular form of voluntary activity, or because they were known to have a particular concern or interest in some important social or political problem.

These specialist consultations, of which nearly thirty have been held between 1963 and 1969, have normally taken place over a week-end, with an attendance of twenty to forty people. They can be classified as follows:

## 1. Consultations for people engaged in the same occupation

EXAMPLES

*a.* Twenty people with responsible jobs in shops and stores came straight from work one Saturday evening. After a meal they introduced themselves and each in turn spoke about the problems with which they had to cope at work. Before midnight an agenda had been drawn up for Sunday under three headings: personnel problems, political problems and moral problems. It was soon discovered that under each heading matters of Christian principle were raised and there were pointers to the sort of action which as Christians they should take. Twenty-four hours was all too short, but those twenty people began to see the relevance of their faith to their work as they had never done before.

*b.* Thirty social workers met to look at the basic assumptions underlying professional social work in this country and to evaluate them from the Christian point of view. They were helped to do so by a Professor of Philosophy who spoke on 'Conflict of roles' and 'Freedom, responsibility and judgment' and by a Lecturer in social work who spoke on 'Values and practice'. Much of the time was spent in group discussion which raised points which were taken up in succeeding years at consultations on 'The problem of evil in social work' and 'Reconciliation in social work with particular reference to the teaching of St Paul'.

*c.* A consultation for those engaged in education on the relationship between education and society and the impact they have upon one another in the realm of values. This was opened by a Scientist presenting 'The challenge of the next fifty years' and other speakers included the Editor of the local newspaper and the Director of the local repertory company.

## 2. Consultations for people in allied occupations

EXAMPLES

*a.* Ten teachers, ten social workers and ten clergymen spent thirty-six hours together considering how, in their three different professions, they went about helping people in need. At the beginning, representatives of each group described their approach to people and the quality and purpose of the professional relationships they sought to make. This was followed by separate discussions of case records of situations in which families were in need of help. Divergences of approach were thus clarified and the way to more effective co-operation made plainer.

*b.* Doctors, clergy and social workers spent a week-end on the ministry to people suffering from bereavement. They learnt much from discussion among themselves and from listening to two outsiders who were brought in because of special studies they had made on the subject.

## 3. Consultations on social problems

EXAMPLES

*a.* A consultation on 'Law and Order' attended by over forty magistrates, lawyers, social workers, head teachers and clergy.

Discussions were opened by a sociologist, a marriage guidance counsellor, a magistrate, a probation officer, a psychiatrist and the Chief Constable. The first session on the final morning began with a theologian's comments on what had gone before. Arising from this consultation a further week-end was arranged on the subject of 'Guilt and guilt feelings'.

*b.* A consultation on 'Town planning and people' to assess the effects upon people and upon community life of recent developments in the fields of re-housing and town planning and to consider the implications of these developments for the social services, the churches, etc. Papers for discussion were presented by a local MP, a sociologist from the Ministry of Housing, a child psychiatrist, a town planning officer, a member of the Town Planning Committee and a lecturer from the Department of Architecture at the University. One result of the consultation was a meeting some months later of architects, planners and teachers to consider education for visual awareness.

*c.* A consultation on 'Broadcasting and the mass media' to assess the effect upon people and on community life of developments in television, sound radio and other forms of mass communication and to consider the implications of these developments for the life of Sheffield, in its various aspects. Over forty educationalists, social workers and clergy attended and discussed papers by a Professor of Adult Education, the Secretary of the Television Research Committee and a Producer with BBC Television. A final session was devoted to the potentialities of local broadcasting.

*d.* A consultation on 'British Industry and Overseas Development' to consider industry's responsibility for the development of the economies of the emerging countries of Asia and Africa. This was attended by twenty industrialists with overseas connections. Expert information was provided by a Civil Servant from the Ministry of Overseas Development and an Economist from the University. The viewpoint of the emerging countries was given by spokesmen from Ghana and Uganda. A member of the Christian Aid staff commented on the moral and theological issues.

## 4. Consultations on cultural themes

EXAMPLES

*a.* A consultation to explore the possibilities of a religious dimension in modern secular painting. Original works were exhibited by a sculptor and an abstract painter, who attempted to describe their own experience of artistic creation. Contemporary trends such as Dada and Pop were interpreted by a University lecturer and parallels discovered in the New Theology. It was the agnostics present who asked for the discussion to be carried further.

*b.* A consultation on 'Man in contemporary art, architecture, drama and theology'. In this case a theologian gave the opening and closing talks. An architect spoke on 'Man and environment' and a fine art lecturer on 'The artist and society'. A lecturer in English and the Director of the Playhouse spoke on drama and the contemporary theatre. There was discussion throughout of comparisons and contrasts.

*c.* A consultation to discover the relationship between musical experience and religious experience and the impact of music upon individuals and society. After an opening talk on music as a means of communication and as a spiritual experience, a Professor of Music discussed inter-relationships between concert music, jazz, folk and pop in the world today and a composer described his own approach to his work. All this was illustrated by records and recordings.

### Some comments on method

Experience has proved that the value of a consultation depends to a large extent upon the preparatory work done beforehand. The normal pattern of such work has been as follows:

1. *Choice of subject.* Almost without exception this has arisen from requests or suggestions made to the Secretary or from discussions in which he has been involved. It has not been thought up by, for instance, an Adult Education Committee.

2. *Planning group.* The first step has usually been to get together a small working party or planning group made up of people interested in the proposed subject from different angles. This has often met several times before even a skeleton programme emerged. It has shared responsibility with the Secretary in deciding whom should be invited to the consultation and in appointing a chairman, group leaders, rapporteur, etc.

3. *Invitations.* A list has been drawn up of people to be invited and personal letters of invitation sent out. In compiling the list help has been sought in the most appropriate quarters; for example, in deciding whom to invite to the 'Law and Order' consultation advice was obtained from the Chairman and Clerk to the local

magistrates, the Secretary of the local Law Society, the Chief Probation Officer, the Children's Officer and the Marriage Guidance Council.

4. *Programme.* On most occasions two or three sessions have been devoted to discussion in small groups. It is out of all these that the suggestions for future action have usually arisen.

5. *Report.* A report of each consultation has been prepared as quickly as possible and circulated to all participants.

# 14. A Theological Critique

IT must be clearly understood that what follows is an attempt at theological reflection on *the papers presented in this book*. It is not and cannot be any sort of judgement (theological or other) on the efforts and aims, achievements and failures which lie behind and are the occasion of the papers. On the one hand, as a personal matter and as myself someone wrestling with the problem and calling of the Christian ministry today, I absolutely refuse to even appear to pass judgement on the efforts of my fellows in the same struggle, especially when I do not know them (or most of them) and cannot talk and share with them. On the other hand, and as a general point, what people find the time and skill to say and write about what they are involved in is not the same as that which they are actually involved in. Hence, and I must repeat it, what follows is in no way an evaluation of any of the activities reported on or of the people involved in them.

I turn therefore to commenting on what is actually presented in the various chapters. One of the (doubtless unworthy) thoughts which then arises is that the tone which might not unfairly be detected in many of these reports could be characterized as 'As to the Church—something is wrong, something must be done, let us do something'. One can almost see an advertisement in an agony column which reads 'Have buildings and some bodies—need role'. That is to say that the first question which comes up which both has theological implications and is a challenge to theology is 'who is experimenting with what to what end?' It is not, I think, sufficiently clear at any point in the book why any reasonable or concerned man should bother with experimenting concerning 'the renewal of the Church'.

I hope it is now clear why I wrote my first paragraph. I expect that the authors both of the papers and of the experiments would have very definite answers to this but unless these answers are spelled out and reflected on I doubt if the experiments reported on can be as useful as they should be to others nor whether other experiments yet to be undertaken will be as radical as they should be. I suppose if one *has* a 'Central Hall' one *has* to find a use for it or, at least, that one had better see if one can find a use for it. Unhappily I cannot be quite sure about this and nothing written in the preceding papers helps to remove my uncertainty.

The basic question is, presumably, 'what is the Church?'—i.e. where does it arise and what is its aim? I do not think that it is sufficient to say something like 'the purpose of the Church is to serve men according to their situations and needs without ecclesiastical strings'. (This is not a precise quotation from the preceding chapters but a composite sentence representing one of the answers implied or stated in the material.)

Firstly, if the purpose of the Church is in no way related to 'ecclesiastical strings' in some sense then there is a fundamental confusion or even dishonesty in the situation which had best be cleared up by the abolition of the Church. Of course, we all know what is being got at in a phrase like 'ecclesiastical strings'. 'Ecclesiastical' is being used in a pejorative and not a purely descriptive sense (i.e. 'to do with the church') and 'ecclesiastical strings' are designed to bring it about that acts of service to men in need shall function as bait to fill pews, produce cash-paying membership and generally ensure that those 'helped' will kowtow to 'the Church' as a sacred institution and an authoritarian pronouncer on the issues of life and death. For myself, I have no doubt that all of our churches have from time to time and unconsciously or consciously exploited situations of dominance to support their institutional ego rather than to serve God and man. But at the moment I am concerned with the point that 'abuse does not do away with the proper use' of a corporation, institution or organism or that, alternatively, if it does then that entity should, if possible, cease to exist. Certainly, no one ought to attempt to experiment with a view to its renewal.

Renewal is possible and desirable only if there is a proper use to be revived, renewed and restored. This proper use will have to have something distinctive about it and in so far as it is distinctive of *the Church*, it will be 'ecclesiastical'. It is, of course, open to one to make the pragmatic judgement that the Church is an obsolete institution with no distinctive functions but that it still contains sufficient persons, money and influence to make it worth using for the time being for other purposes independent of it and which will survive beyond it. Some people active in the churches seem in practice to be operating on some such premiss as this and other people outside the churches also seem to treat the churches like this. For example, various leaders in the movements for black liberation on both sides of the Atlantic clearly find the churches very useful institutions for exploiting the guilt-feelings of whites with a view to obtaining at any rate money. This seems to me to be a perfectly legitimate tactic in a political struggle to change the power structures. I further think that the churches have 'asked for it'. But I take it that this book is not concerned with finding a temporary use for the Church nor with getting the most you can out of the Church before it is finally finished.

We are left, therefore, with the question about the proper and distinctive use of the Church. I dwell on this point at some length because I think it has more implications than are always seen. Consider, for example, the oft-used (and, in my opinion, important) notion of 'letting the world set the agenda'. Setting aside for the moment fairly obvious difficulties involved in the use of the phrase (such as, e.g. that it may sometimes be necessary to suggest to 'the world' that an ignored item should be restored to the agenda), I should like to draw attention to a different type of danger in policies licensed by such a phrase. We may let the world set the agenda, or choose from the list of items on the world agenda, in such a way that we can find things for the Church to do which 'justify' the Church's existence or, at least, allow it to continue to exist. In any such case we are not really taking the secular seriously but using it to ensure or make likely the continuation of the Church.

I am afraid that I cannot be as precisely and practically positive here as I would wish but I remain both somewhat uneasy and somewhat baffled when members of church congregations, ministers of churches and, through them, church buildings are found new (and allegedly renewing) roles in fields like social work, community relations and the like. The uneasiness arises from two considerations. The first I have already raised. Is the work really being done for its own sake and therefore being faced up to in its own terms or is it really treated as a new version of 'church work'?

The second consideration looks like the exact opposite of the first but I suspect that the implications to be drawn from both considerations in fact have to be made to converge in both understanding and practice. If we merely find new roles in social fields and social contexts with the agenda set by those fields are we not letting the people concerned down because we are failing to bring into them just that distinctiveness which the Gospel has to offer, or, perhaps, just that distinctive offer which is the Gospel? The dilemma seems to be—without identity no service; without distinctiveness a failure to offer the very service we exist to give. However, the dilemma has to be faced because unless we face it, letting the world set the agenda may involve failing to take the world seriously on both counts. We may use it to keep the Church going and so be failing really to listen to, deal with and be part of the world. On the other hand, we may fail to be the means of offering what might be offered through us to the world at large in its specific reality and need.

Now, a phrase like 'that disinctive offer which is the Gospel' may well be used in an attempt to paper over what is really a cavernous crack in the argument of this so-called 'theological critique'. For part, and a very important part, of that 'something which is wrong with the Church' which has led to the experiments reported on in this book and to the research for renewal, of which they are simply a part, is just that the Church does not seem to have much idea of what is 'that distinctive offer which is the Gospel'. There may continue to be a good deal of talk *inside* the Church about this but the local communities which represent the Church in particular situations do not show many signs, in the communities in which they live, of either receiving or passing on 'a distinctive offer', where the offer is supposed to be plain, practical and powerful good news about the possibilities involved in being human. So there may well be little point in appearing to criticize the reports contained in this book for giving us so little illumination about the *distinctive* role of the Church. The need for the experiments would never have arisen if we already had this illumination or if our ancient illuminations on this score had not now proved insufficient.

This is, therefore, the point in our argument where it should become clearer than ever that a theological critique is not an evaluation or appreciation which in any sense conveys or suggests praise and blame about particular persons and enterprises. The purpose of a theological critique is to help us to see where we are with a view to becoming clearer about where we ought to go or at least to see some ways open to us along which we ought not to go.

I believe that reflection on the chapters in this book does expose the dilemma indicated above and that the way this dilemma is posed to us is a function of the uncertainty about the role of the Church and the uncertainty about the distinctiveness of the Gospel which are themselves interrelated. But the exposure of this dilemma and what lies behind it, far from being a theological *condemnation* of the experiments under review in fact points us towards both the theological *significance* and the theological *justification* of these experiments as well as indicating lines for a continuing theological *criticism* of them and of their like.

In his book *Value Systems and Social Process*, in which he has so many fascinating and illuminating things to say about our present predicaments in living with such rapid and extensive change, Sir Geoffrey Vickers picks up Professor Karl Popper's view of scientific method which 'assumes that all scientific activity starts with a problem' and he goes on to add 'By a problem I understand the felt need to remove some disparity thrown up by the appreciative system . . .' (p. 199). This understanding of a problem leading to methodical investigation with a view not only to solving the problem but to thereby making new discoveries seems to me to be very illuminating with regard to the situation of the Church and to the need for, and purpose of, experiments such as those described in this book.

In the case of all of us associated with the book, our 'appreciative system' is, we hope, deeply affected by our commitment to Jesus Christ, our understanding and hopes of the Christian faith, our membership of and loyalty to the Christian Church. Within our mutually shared (although not precisely identical) Christian appreciative systems the Church, in its actual manifestation in particular situations, constitutes a problem. There manifestly is a 'disparity' between what the Church can be seen to be doing, trying to do and failing to do (and between what the Church can be seen to be, trying to be and failing to be) and the commitment, faith and hope kindled by Jesus Christ. We are often alerted to this fundamental disparity by various simple examples of malfunctioning (empty buildings, failure to get any response in budget-raising, contempt for *Church* representation with regard to a pressing local issue, etc., etc.). The manifest disparity which produces the felt need and constitutes the problem is clear enough although there may be great difficulty in spelling out an agreed diagnosis, involving agreed uses of agreed theological terminology, of the functional mismatch between what the Church actually is in a particular community and what it should be (or should at least be trying to be). That is, we may well not be able to start on the problem from much more than a recognition of its existence (through our 'feeling a need') and the formulation 'something is wrong with the Church, something must be done' which I implicitly criticized at the beginning of this chapter. Clearly the Church (i.e. a particular local manifestation of the Church) is practically useless as it is and therefore uses have to be found for it.

But what has to be recognized is that the experiment (each and all of the experiments) is about *everything* and that everything is *in question*. A problem which is thrown up within an appreciative system is also a problem for and about that appreciative system. And the problem of the Church concretized in the problems of these particular churches, both arises from and raises questions for the way we understand and are to understand the Church, the Gospel, Christian faith, worship, community, obedience, etc., etc.

It may be shattering to recognize this. Initially it would seem that for many people it is. Eventually it is liberating. In any case it is inevitable. For any reflection on the theological problems which come up once you are forced to experiment and then have results to consider will always produce some dilemma such as I have formulated above or else some other formulation of the problems which makes it equally clear that all the parts of the problems inter-act with one another and that therefore all are in question.

Hence the theological significance of the experiments discussed in this book is that they reflect the only method available to us of seeking a renewal both in our understanding of the Gospel and of our obedient structuring of the Church in our present circumstances of uncertainty, of mismatch between the churches and society, and of mismatch between the churches and the Gospel they exist to embody. The various uncertainties and the various mismatches both follow from and contribute to one another. (e.g. We have got the shape of the Church wrong because we have failed to understand the Gospel appropriately to that Gospel and to our day and age but, at the same time, we cannot understand either the Gospel or our day and age properly because we have the shape of the Church wrong—and so on.)

So we cannot 'put the Church straight' by *first* 'going back to theological first principles'. The 'crookedness' of the Church has already distorted either our theological first principles or, at least, our capacity to understand them aright. Conversely, however, we shall not 'get the Church straight' either simply by finding a role or roles for it whereby it will fit functionally into society or by getting a viable use for its present plant, building and personnel *without* reference to theological principles. For unless the Church is embodying, in its particular community expressions within the larger community, some distinctive reference then the only honest and human thing to do is to dissolve the Church, either at once or with the minimum period of phased obsolescence, into the other institutions of society. Further, however, we shall not rediscover in practice and with power *what* the distinctive reference of the Church is and *how* it works distinctively unless and until we have worked for some time, more or less in the dark, at the sort of practical and rule of thumb attempts *both* to discover the Churches' role today (How does it 'fit' into society?) *and* to discover its distinctive contribution (How does it 'stand out' in relation to society?) of which the experiments reported in the previous chapters are various sorts of more or less successful and more or less balanced examples.

My suspicion is that many of the experiments, at least as reported, tend to lack balance in the direction of being concerned very much more with finding a use for what there is and with fitting in to society and very much less with seeking to make a distinctive contribution to society and to re-discover the point and power of the Gospel. However, even if this suspicion is justified, my foregoing analysis should help to make it clear that this is the sort of imbalance we should expect at this initial stage of experimentation concerning Gospel, Church and Society. The purpose of exposing the imbalance is to assist in the evaluation of experimentation so far in relation to planning further experiments. In this connection, I would particularly suggest that one result of this imbalance is to make the experiments and the reflection upon them very much less radical (and therefore less experimental) than the situation demands. It is comparatively easy to adjust a bit and find *a* job for people, plants and funds in relation to their environment and to their (slightly refurbished) understanding of themselves. It is much more difficult to move structures and attitudes in a direction which will expose people to a real renewal which will make a distinctive difference both in our understanding of the Church and of our Christian role in society.

However, once again, we cannot expect really productive and creative results of experimentation at the beginning of our experiments. Further, we have to start from where we are and, as more than one writer in this book has pointed out, if you attempt to move too far and too fast away from 'where you are' you lose even the people and the resources you have got as the base and basis for the experimentation and eventual renewal. Here we return to the question of the theological significance of this type of experimentation and of this type of understanding of the experimental situation. It is going to take a great deal of patient, tough and loving work to get a real understanding within the Church of our real situation. Much of what I have been saying above will seem to many people (even if they can follow it!) to be something like a 'betrayal of Christ and the Gospel' rather than a faithful search for renewal based on a strong trust in and conviction about the power of Jesus and His Gospel. Hence the need to develop further, and therefore to express more simply, the whole theological significance of this enterprise. We have got to teach congregations, committees and ourselves to see clearly the inter-connexion and feed-back between mis-understanding of the Gospel, mis-structuring of the churches and mis-match with local communities. And all this will have to be seen as a strong challenge and invitation to faith in God the Holy Spirit as Transcendence at work in the midst to move us forward experimentally to the renewal on all fronts that we seek and need.

An important tool in furthering our experimentation and in developing our theological awareness is the undertaking and use of more or less systematic area surveys and assessments of locality needs, such as are referred to in several of the chapters. But the tool can easily be badly forged and very badly used. In my under-standing, and in the context of the type of experiments and of experimentation we are discussing here, the role of such a survey (however amateurishly carried out) is to deepen (or perhaps even to initiate) a realistic understanding by the church community of the community in which the church body exists and of the actual relationship between the church community and the wider com-munity. They function therefore in illuminating the mismatch be-tween the Church community and the local community at large. They do not directly throw any light on how the Church is to understand the Gospel and to serve the larger community in the light of that understanding.

Unless we are clear about this we shall simply be finding the Church a temporary job in, for example, stopping some gaps in social services as they are currently conceived and we shall fail to begin on the task of seeking the distinctive renewal of the Church for distinctive service. In any case it is clear that all surveys start with presuppositions about 'needs' which already imply views about man, society, what it is to live satisfactorily and so on. If they are to play a part in experimentation which is theologically significant they must eventually be used in such a way as to chal-lenge all these presuppositions and to raise questions about the resources which are available to meet the 'needs' which are exposed or the deeper needs of which the currently diagnosed 'needs' are either symptoms or misunderstandings. In particular we have to face the fundamental fact that no amount of 'help' to meet however many 'needs', even if it were available without limit, would finally meet the needs of men, women and children, individually and in society. What men finally 'need' to be is themselves and no one can ultimately 'be themselves' for anyone else. Hence there is a fundamental question about how men and women can take on responsibility for and participation in meeting our 'needs' (if the approach is in terms of 'need') which has always to be borne in mind and very frequently raised. A 'survey of local needs' can be just as much as prelude to a new form of paternalism as it can be a prelude to a new form of church work.

But such surveys can be very useful as a means of shaking a church congregation or congregations into a realistic awareness of their present uselessness and isolation. They may then, via reflection on the survey, find one or two immediate but temporary tasks to perform. It is necessary to be very clear that these 'uses' which are thereby found for church members, and perhaps church buildings, however valid they may be in themselves in the short term, are simply steps on the way back to discovering the distinctive use, contribution and existence of the Church. In order to get back to this the Church must be living in society and getting to grips with reality as it is locally manifested. But there is no theological sense or virtue in being *reduced* to the level of the needs, evaluations and expectations of society *without remainder*. We must hope and look for the newness which we believe God has for all men and so for us through Jesus. On the other hand we certainly do have to be on the way to learning full identification before we can be open to receive such newness.

Thus I would argue that the theological *justification* of the experimental method reflected in the experiments reported in this book is retained as long as we understand their theological *significance* along the lines I have been attempting to outline and see the need for constant theological *criticism*. The criticism is designed to keep the proper creative and questioning balance between (1) finding uses for fitting available church resources into society, (2) worrying about the connection between those uses and the understanding we so far have of the Gospel from and for which the church lives and, (3) criticizing the uses we are finding for the Church in the light of our understanding of the Gospel and vice versa. Thus we shall not settle down to a slightly modified pattern of 'usefulness' but may be put on our way to being converted ourselves and to being a really converting and disturbing element in society.

It seems to me pretty clear, as I have already hinted, that if we pursue this type of experimentation as it should be pursued then we shall find that we are on to something which is deeply and creatively explosive, both theologically and institutionally. In order to be distinctive in and for society we shall probably have to give up most of the things that render us distinctive (but as an obsolescent institution) at the moment. For example, we shall probably become more and more conscious of ourselves as the Church (i.e. people united together by a common call of God and commitment to Jesus) but have less and less use for distinctive buildings. We shall find more and more need for ministering (putting together elements of the human situation and insights of the Gospel) but shall probably find a need for fewer full-time ministers. We shall become much more concerned with hearing or discovering the Word of God in the sense of finding new ways forward through our human and social dilemmas but we shall find much less use for preaching. We shall become more and more dependent on our fellowship with one another and our participation in common enterprises but we shall have much less formal 'coming-together' in our church programmes. We shall find ourselves much more deeply committed to working out patterns of common action and so facing the realities of moral judgement and action but shall neither expect nor encourage ethical pronouncements from our church authorities. All this will, perhaps, go along with the growth of a much stronger (but probably much less frequently visible) church fellowship, a rediscovery of the Christian tradition as a living source of sustenance, provocation and illumination for living with today's questions, and a renewed sense of the worship of God as the Lord who offers a salvation which is a constant power for wholeness and a constant hope of wholeness.

But if it is asked 'And what does all *that* mean?' the reply must be 'We shall have to experiment in the hope that God will enable us to find out'. For the chief thing which can be said theologically about what is reported in this book is not that the people concerned 'went too far' but rather that they have certainly not gone far enough. May we not, however, be thankful that some people have had the courage to make a start?